Eton College in the Victorian Age

Boys, masters, parents and dames in the context of broader social change

H. A. SHIRWANI

Table of Contents

1. Introduction

How did Eton College fare amid the tides of change sweeping through England over the course of Queen Victoria's reign? Social histories of Victorian England have identified a number of trends at work: the rise of the middle classes;[1] the revolution in transport and communications;[2] secularisation;[3] professionalisation (of medicine, education, the army and the civil service);[4] the ideal of domesticity;[5] the

---

[1]   John Tosh, *A Man's Place: Masculinity and the Middle-Class Home in Victorian England* (New Haven and London: Yale University Press, 2007), p. 46.

[2]   T. W. Bamford, *Rise of the public schools: a study of boys' public boarding schools in England and Wales from 1837 to the present day* (London: Nelson, 1967), p. 60.

[3]   Hugh McLeod, *Secularisation in Western Europe, 1848–1914.* (Basingstoke: Macmillan, 2000).

[4]   Harold Perkin, *The Rise of the Professional Society: England since 1880* (London: Routledge, 2003), p. xii.

cult of empire;[6] and the family becoming an affectional base even as it became physically dispersed.[7]

These trends provide the context for another Victorian phenomenon: the expansion of the public schools.[8] A public school can be defined as an endowed senior school that attracted (male) pupils from all over the country. (A 'private school' at this time was one that was privately owned by an individual.) The desire of the increasingly prosperous middle classes to secure a prestigious education for their sons resulted in the opening of several new public schools from the 1840s onwards and rising numbers for the more established schools.[9] By the

---

[5]   Tosh, *A Man's Place*, pp. 13-14.

[6]   James Anthony Mangan, *Athleticism in the Victorian and Edwardian Public School: The emergence and consolidation of an educational ideology* (London: Routledge, 2012).

[7]   John R. Gillis, *A World of Their Own Making: Myth, Ritual, and the Quest for Family Values* (Harvard: Harvard University Press, 1997), p. 71.

[8]   Edward C. Mack, *Public Schools and British Opinion Since 1860: The Relationship between Contemporary Ideas and the Evolution of an English Institution* (New York: Columbia University Press, 1941), p. 4.

[9]   Jonathan Gathorne-Hardy, *The public school phenomenon, 597-1977* (London : Hodder and Stoughton, 1977), pp. 105-113.

second half of the nineteenth century, it became a consensus that the characteristics and qualifications of a successful gentleman could only be acquired through a public school education.[10] Attending a public school became associated with social status, and the term 'public school' itself became a coveted badge of prestige. For all these reasons, an increasing number of English families felt their boys ought to spend much of their adolescence within the community of a public school such as Eton.[11]

What effects did these social, cultural and technological developments have upon Eton? This short study will seek to answer this question in three ways. First, it will analyse how Eton changed as a physical space over the Victorian period (Chapter 2). Then it will look at the roles played by different members of the community within that space (Chapter 3). Finally, it will seek to discern the ethos of

---

[10]   Honey, *Tom Brown's Universe* (1977), p. 146.

[11]   Vivian Ogilvie, *The English Public School* (London: Batsford, 1957), pp. 139-179; John Honey, *Tom Brown's Universe: The Development of the Victorian Public School* (London: Millington, 1977), pp. 238-247.

this community (Chapter 4).

Chapter 2 ('Places') and Chapter 3 ('People') will study surface changes, focusing on differences between Eton as it was under the headmastership of Edward Craven Hawtrey (1834-1853) and what the school became under the headmastership of Edmond Warre, (1884-1905). Chapter 4 ('Values') will move up to a more abstract level and analyse the various competing values within the school community, using the *Eton College Chronicle* as a source and focusing on changes between the start and end of the headmastership of Edmond Warre. It will become apparent that some changes were due to local and internal factors, but that many more were due to the broader trends affecting the whole of English society.

Appendices A-F contain data referred to in the text, though they can stand alone as items of interest. For example, a comparison of the lists of masters in Appendix D and Appendix E will reveal particular ways in which the school had and had not changed over the course of the Victorian period.

Readers who are interested in a broader historiographical understanding can refer to the note in Appendix G, which covers the historical debates this study responds to, as well as the sources and methods used.

Finally, it should be noted that this is a focused study of developments at Eton College over a hundred years ago. The Eton of today has undergone many substantial changes, even if aspects of it retain a connection with the past. Comments within this study refer only to the Eton of the Victorian period.

2. Places: Victorian Eton as a Space

2.1 A Guided Tour of Eton[12]

To visit Eton is to walk through a trail of changes experienced by the Victorians. A visitor can take a train from London to one of two railway stations in Windsor. Both opened in 1849, much later than the surrounding network, after two decades of opposition from Eton College based on fears that the railway would disrupt the discipline of the school.[13] On arrival, the visitor can cross a bridge over the Thames into Eton. Walking down Eton High Street, the first College-related building to be seen is the

---

[12]   See Appendix A: A Map of Modern Eton.

[13]   Debbie Keenan and Bobbie Latter, *Windsor: A History* (Salisbury: Francis Frith, 2004), pp. 63-65; C. R. Potts, *Windsor to Slough: A Royal Branch Line* (Oxford: The Oakwood Press, 1993), pp. 7-13.

Sanatorium on the left. Proposals had been made for such a facility since the plagues of the seventeenth century, but it was only at the start of the Victorian period that action was taken.[14]

Soon, the original buildings of Henry VI's foundation will loom into view, including the Chapel and accommodation for seventy boys on scholarships ('Collegers'). In various side streets, the visitor will see some very large houses, five or more windows along. These are boarding houses for the non-scholarship boys who live in the town ('Oppidans'), whom Eton began accepting shortly after its foundation as a way of increasing revenue.[15] The visitor will notice that the Oppidan houses are roughly equal in size if not in style. This is the result of a centralisation and standardisation process begun in the Victorian period, by the end of which most of these previously privately owned and independently run boarding houses had fallen under the ownership and

---

[14]   John Briscoe, '555 years of Medical Care at Eton' (unpublished lecture, ECA, 1996), pp. 1-3.

[15]   H. C. Maxwell Lyte, *A History of Eton College 1440-1910* (London: Macmillan, 1911), pp. 155-157.

management of the College.[16]

As for the scholars' accommodation, the authorities had long tolerated a disparity in the living conditions between the wealthy, fee-paying Oppidans and the relatively poor Collegers, most of whom were locked at night into one large room.[17] The current scholars' accommodation, with individual rooms as in Oppidan houses, owes much to improvements in 1846.[18] To see the scholars' accommodation, the Chapel and other foundation buildings, the visitor will pass by School Office. This is the hub of non-financial school administration and was built at the very end of the Victorian period, to be presided over by a School Clerk.[19] At the start of the Victorian period, the head master had been expected to

---

[16]   L. S. R. Byrne and E.L. Churchill, *Changing Eton: A Survey of Conditions based on the History of Eton since the Royal Commision of 1862-64* (London, Jonathan Cape, 1937), p. 130.

[17]   Francis St. John Thackery, *Memoir of Edward Craven Hawtrey* (London: George Bell and Sons 1896), p. 81.

[18]   Ibid., p. 82.

[19]   C. R. L. Fletcher, *Edmond Warre* (London: John Murray, 1922), p. 149.

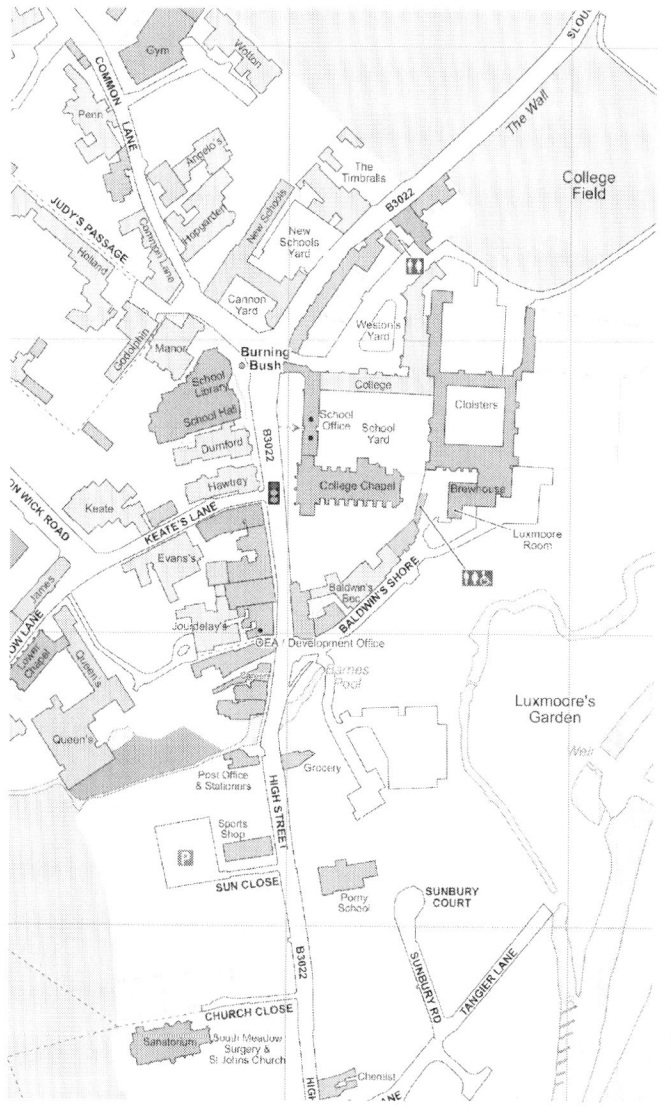

undertake by himself such administrative matters as there were, possibly with the help of his butler.[20] Above School Office is Upper School, a hall which contains the names of several notable Old Etonians, and it is striking to see the clusters of old boys grouped by family. The practice of families identifying with a school became particularly pronounced in the Victorian age; it was something the men of the family could have in common amid the dislocations of a modernising world, in which scions of even the most established dynasties might have to travel far from the family home to seek a living, with no guarantee that it would not have been sold off by the time they returned.[21]

Across the road from the foundation buildings are a large hall and a domed library. These are dedicated to the memory of Old Etonians who died in the Boer War. The fact that non-religious buildings were used for a memorial points to the secularisation of life throughout the Victorian

---

[20]   Thackery, p. 87.

[21]   Honey, *Tom Brown's Universe*, p. 162.

period.[22] Beyond the library, is Cannon Yard. This is surrounded by schoolrooms, including New Schools, which were the first 'modern' classrooms (built 1861-1876) outside the original foundation buildings.[23] These were built in order to accommodate the broadening curriculum, which by this stage included mathematics and modern languages, in addition to the traditional Latin and Greek.[24] In the middle of Cannon Yard is a real cannon, caught at the Battle of Sebastopol and donated to Eton in 1867.[25] This is fitting, as it was after the debacles of the Crimean War that reforms of the army and civil service were implemented, including entrance examinations.[26] Families could no longer rely solely on connections as examinations had to be passed, hence Eton adapting its curriculum and building these new schoolrooms.[27]

Walking past Cannon Yard and New Schools,

---

[22]   Fletcher, *Warre*, p. 145.

[23]   R. Austen-Leigh, *A Guide to Eton College* (Eton: Eton College, 1988), p. 106.

[24]   Byrne and Churchill, pp. 37-39.

[25]   Austen-Leigh, p. 107.

[26]   Mangan, *Athleticism*, p. 13.

[27]   French and Rothery, p. 240.

the visitor will be able to follow the Slough Road up to the school playing fields, which the school began to acquire from the middle of the Victorian period onwards. It was towards the end of the Victorian period that a school-wide games programme was instituted, becoming central to the late Victorian cult of games, manliness and empire, even if their most immediate benefit was keeping the ever-increasing school population supervised and occupied.[28]

Our visitor has thus seen many traces of the nineteenth-century trends that Eton had to contend with: the railway revolution;[29] professionalisation (of medicine, education, the army and the civil service);[30] the ideals of domesticity and privacy;[31] the closer supervision of children;[32] the family becoming an affectional base even as it became physically

---

[28]   Mangan, *Athleticism*, p. 68.

[29]   Bamford , p. 60.

[30]   Harold Perkin, *The Rise of the Professional Society: England since 1880* (London: Routledge, 2003), p. xii.

[31]   Tosh, *A Man's Place*, pp. 13-14.

[32]   Ibid., p. 60.

dispersed;[33] secularisation;[34] and the cults of games and empire.[35] Common to many of these is the broader rise of the middle classes, which affected all aspects of Victorian England, including, the visitor may note, even this most aristocratic of institutions.[36]

Having introduced the key Victorian developments within the landscape of Eton, and linked them to broader trends, this chapter will now carry out a comparative analysis of certain features of the landscape as they were at the start and end of the Victorian period. The analysis will make use of documents produced within Eton, be they primary sources or commentary by members of the Eton community. It will be shown that Eton changed considerably, being in no way immune to the broader trends sweeping through the country.

---

[33] John R. Gillis, *A World of Their Own Making: Myth, Ritual, and the Quest for Family Values* (Harvard: Harvard University Press, 1997), p. 71.

[34] Hugh McLeod, *Secularisation in Western Europe, 1848–1914.* (Basingstoke: Macmillan, 2000).

[35] Mangan, *Athleticism.*

[36] Tosh, *A Man's Place*, p. 46.

2.2 Travelling to and from Eton: Transport

At the start of the Victorian period, boys travelled to Eton by coach. This changed with the building of Windsor station in October 1849 and then Riverside station in December 1849. One can imagine that this was a tense time for the College authorities. Their objections to the coming of the railway, and the supposed risk of 'getting the boys into Vice', had finally been overruled by Parliament after a sustained campaign by local notables, such as the editor of the *Windsor Express* and the Dean of Windsor, who wanted their town to reap the commercial advantages of train travel.[37]

A letter of November 1849 reveals how ill disposed yet increasingly resigned the College authorities were to the railway revolution. In this letter, head master Edward Hawtrey complains to the

---

[37] Potts, pp. 13 and 29.

head of the Great Western railway that the staff at Slough station had allowed a boy seeking to flee Eton, on his own, and without money, to board a train.[38] Having upbraided the company for undermining school discipline, Hawtrey reminds it of Eton's 'Privilege allowed by the Act which established the Slough Station': the presence of policemen working for the College but paid by the company.

Hawtrey's tone conveys a sense of the old order demanding the respect of the arriviste commercial and professional classes. The fact that Eton has not proceeded with the supervisory arrangements permitted by the act is further indication of this aristocratic hauteur, as it feels it should not be tasked with such matters. However, Hawtrey does go into some detail about the provisions of the act and the theoretical procedures in place. This is a sign of Eton having to engage with the forces of technological, economic and administrative change that were affecting all areas of English society. Engaging with these broader forces of change was

---

[38]   ECA, COLL/P13/22.

clearly affecting Eton's own procedures and policies. In that sense, Hawtrey, despite his status as an educator of gentlemen, is revealing himself to be a middle class professional communicating with another middle class professional. His resigned engagement with a new administrative burden indicates the beginnings of a change in working practices.

By the end of the Victorian period, these working practices had become thoroughly professionalised, as evidenced by the mass of administrative documents found in the papers of the head master at the time, Edmond Warre. These show that Eton was able to adopt three terms with precise start and end times, rather than two halves with much leeway for delayed arrival. Furthermore, the school now engaged in a growing list of sports fixtures. All of this would have been unthinkable when boys relied on coach travel.[39]

The spread of the railways and the rise of the public schools are two Victorian phenomena that

---

[39]   ECA, COLL P/05.

went hand in hand.[40] In the case of Eton, the railways can be seen to have affected it in two principal ways. Firstly, they brought many more boys to Eton, with enrolment almost doubling, from 519 in 1830 to 1027 in 1900. The railways also helped bring the bourgeois world to Eton's doorstep and obliged the school to take part, helping bring about the greater professionalisation to be found at the end of the Victorian period.

2.3 Living at Eton: Accommodation

At the start of the Victorian period, fee-paying Oppidans lodged in local boarding houses and were able to secure all comforts that their parents could afford. The Eton authorities were conscious that the Collegers' accommodation was, by comparison, unsatisfactory. For example, on an 1842 visit to Eton, the King of Prussia wished to see how Henry VI's foundationers lived but was denied access.[41] A subscription was raised and the New Buildings were

---

[40]   Bamford, p. 60.

[41]   Thackery, p. 92.

unveiled in 1846.[42] The feeling that even the lower class scholars were entitled to improved quarters and better food reflect the broader celebration of home life which was on the rise in England at this time.[43] Indeed, there had been calls for this sort of reform for some time. An 1834 pamphlet devoted most of its content to supporting the conservation of all practices at Eton, religious and educational, exactly as they were. Having established its conservative credentials, it goes on to argue that one area of Eton life is in urgent need of reform: the living conditions of Collegers. Moreover, the arguments put forward are premised on the virtue of personal privacy and its association with propriety.[44] These values are at the centre of the middle-class ideal of the home described

---

[42]   Ibid., p. 80.

[43]   Tosh, 'Domesticity and Manliness in the Victorian Middle Class: The family of Edward White Benson' in *Manful Assertions: Masculinities in Britain since 1800* ed. by Michael Roper and John Tosh (London: Routledge, 1991) p. 44; Tosh, *A Man's Place*, pp. 13-14.

[44]   *The Eton system of education vindicated, and its capabilities of improvement considered, in reply to some recent publications* (Bristol Selected Pamphlets, 1834).

in detail by Davidoff and Hall.[45]

By the close of the Victorian period, much
had changed again. Almost all the local boys'
boarding houses had been purchased by the school
and the system was overseen by the head master.[46]
The improvement and the increasingly centralized
administration of boys' accommodation reflected the
broader trends of domesticity and professionalisation
which were central to the rise of the middle classes.
This is an example of the need to distinguish between
rhetoric and reality. Much of the discourse
surrounding boys' education was evocative of the
'flight from domesticity'.[47] Tosh argues that this
became evident as the home came to be identified as
a female-dominated space, with men seeking a refuge
in all-male worlds. This phenomenon is apparent in
much of the discourse emanating from Eton towards
the end of the 19th century, some of which will be
analysed in Chapter 4. Suffice it to say for the present

---

[45]   Davidoff and Hall, pp. 357-396.

[46]   Byrne and Churchill, p. 270.

[47]   Tosh, 'Domesticity and Manliness in the Victorian Middle
Class', p. 67.

that, while the discourse shied away from the notion of domesticity, that very notion was present in all the changes on the ground detailed above.

2.4 Soul, Body and Mind at Eton: Chapel, Sanatorium and Memorial Buildings

Although the body of Eton expanded and reformed throughout the Victorian period, the Chapel remained at its heart. Certain developments may give cause to think that Eton was becoming more religious over the course of the period. Hawtrey's biographer says that 'Chapel services were certainly the least satisfactory feature of Eton in Hawtrey's time and long afterwards', causing 'listlessness, inattention, sometimes even irreverence'.[48] That system continued into the 1860s and 'it required a Parliamentary Commission to give it its coup de grace'.[49] From the 1860s onwards the chapel services were better regulated and, at times, more frequent than before. In 1891, a second place of worship, Lower Chapel, was

---

[48]   Thackery, pp. 94-95.

[49]   Ibid., p. 95.

opened.[50] This development is primarily an indication of the growth in pupil numbers over the course of the Victorian period. In addition, it is indicative of the authorities' desire to incorporate all of these pupils into the religious life of the school, as well as their increasing professionalism in effecting the changes required to achieve this. However, there were broader changes afoot which indicate that, overall, Eton was subject to the tides of secularisation that were sweeping throughout the country. These were reflected in one building project that took place under Hawtrey at the start of the Victorian period and another that took place under Warre towards its end.

The building of the Sanatorium in 1844 may not initially seem to betoken a process of secularisation. It is clear from an 1842 circular to parents that Hawtrey was minded to improve arrangements for the boys' health and saw this project as the most efficient way of achieving this.[51] The fact that Hawtrey felt a duty of care to the boys and acted upon it in this way is a

---

[50]   Austen-Leigh, p. 122.

[51]   ECA, COLL/P13/20

sign of Eton responding to changing notions of childcare, which had been influenced by the middle-class domestic ideal. Furthermore, it is a reflection of the creeping professionalisation of working methods at Eton (with Hawtrey going into detail about his consultations with architects and 'experienced London Physicians'). However, it can also be seen as Hawtrey broadening the school's responsibilities to include not just teaching and the curacy of souls, but also looking to the boys' physical welfare. Moreover, the presence of a Sanatorium would bring with it medical professionals, who would become resident authority figures, albeit representing a more modern and worldly realm of expertise than the clerics that had so far dominated Eton.[52] These medical professionals did not preach or teach, but their very presence showed that Eton was opening up to trends which were ultimately at odds with the religious direction that had thus far been its mainstay.

At the very end of the Victorian period, Warre proposed a memorial to the 129 Etonians who died in

---

[52]   Briscoe, pp. 1-3.

the Boer War. The result was a complex of buildings on the opposite side of the High Street to the Chapel. Work began shortly after the end of Queen Victoria's reign. School Hall, built to seat 1,200, was opened in 1908. The new School Library, a domed octagon, was opened in 1910. [53] The fact that non-religious buildings were designated as memorials for the war dead, shows the even deeper influence of secularisation at Eton by the end of the Victorian period. Previous to this, an act of commemoration would have been religious and therefore associated with the Chapel. The position of these buildings directly opposite the buildings of Henry VI foundation, represents an alternative and a counterweight, if not a challenge, to the religious direction for which the school was established.

It can therefore be seen how the addition of new buildings, from the Sanatorium to School Hall, showed that religion was no longer the principal conduit for the community. Indeed, whereas the Chapel could no longer hold the entire population of

---

[53]   Austen-Leigh, pp. 134-136.

the school, the secular School Hall could accommodate everyone present at the school at the time of its construction.

2.5 Teaching at Eton: Schoolrooms

At the start of the Victorian period, all teaching took place within the confines of the foundation buildings. The one exception was mathematics. It had been introduced as a supplementary subject in 1836, with boys who chose it attending lessons in the Rotunda, a large building at the other end of Eton, reflecting the subject's outsider status. Its construction had to be paid for by the Head of Mathematics (the head master's cousin, Stephen Hawtrey – another candidate had turned down the post on learning of its conditions). His assistants were forbidden from wearing gowns and from addressing any complaints about boys directly to the head master.[54]

By the end of the Victorian period, all this had

---

[54]   Thackery, pp. 88-89.

changed. Mathematics teachers had been incorporated as full members of staff and the curriculum was gradually broadened. This, together with increasing pupil numbers had resulted in the building of new school rooms: New Schools, a large complex of modern school rooms, was built between 1861 and 1876; a laboratory and music room were built in 1869; work on the New Mathematical Schools was begun in 1875; the School of Mechanics was built in 1879; and work on the Science Schools was begun in 1881.

These building projects reflect a number of developments that were sweeping through Eton. These new schoolrooms were required to accommodate rising pupil numbers, part of a national trend that, from the 1840s onwards, had seen the building of several new public schools to accommodate the desire of an increasingly prosperous middle classes to secure a prestigious education for their sons.[55] The fact that the new school room buildings were dedicated to particular subjects

---

[55]   Mack, vol. II, p. 4.

represents a broadening of curriculum and an increase in the teaching staff, including various specialists in mathematics, sciences, and modern languages.[56]

This broadening of the curriculum reflected another trend at work in English society, which was credentialisation. At the start of the Victorian, period wealthy families could rely on connections to secure employment for their sons. By the end of the Victorian period, the army, the universities, and the civil service were setting entrance exams. The personal networks retained their influence, but there were now exams to be passed, and schools, including Eton, responded accordingly through changes in the curriculum.[57]

2.6 Games and other activities at Eton: Beyond the schoolroom

If the Duke of Wellington ever said that the Battle of Waterloo was won on the fields of Eton,

---

[56]   Byrne and Churchill, pp. 37-39.

[57]   French and Rothery, p. 240.

this was not a reference to sport. When the Duke was at Eton, the surrounding fields were principally the scene of fights, poaching expeditions, and other unsupervised escapades.[58] Games, such as they existed, were entirely boy-run and masters took no interest when they tolerated them at all. It was only towards the end of the Victorian period that a school-wide games programme was instituted. Regardless of educators' rhetoric about building character, this policy was first and foremost a means of social control. In research on a range of public schools, Mangan has found evidence of headmasters bringing in compulsory games towards the end of the 19th century as a solution to increasing pupil numbers. Although there is no founding document for such a programme in the Eton College Archives, the way in which Warre and his colleagues gradually took over boys' games initially as coaches and later as organisers, is in line with developments at the schools studied by Mangan, especially Harrow and

---

[58]   Norman Vance, 'The Ideal of Manliness' in *The Victorian Public School: Studies in the Development of an Educational Institution* ed. by Brian Simon and Ian Bradley (Dublin: Gill and Macmillan, 1975), pp. 115-128 (p. 116).

Marlborough. [59]

Finally, by the end of the Victorian period boys were taking part in a number of activities which, at the start of the period, had either been boy-run or not existed at all. Foremost amongst these were the Eton College Rifle Volunteers, which reflected the growing militarism of the time.[60] Music was formalised with more teachers and facilities.[61] Drama, which had flourished at the start of the Victorian period, albeit in an informal fashion, was actually banned by Warre.[62] This could be understood as an attempt to assert a vision of masculinity which precluded amateur theatricals. All of these activities were reported in some detail in another new phenomenon, the *Eton College Chronicle*, which will be analysed in detail in

---

[59]   Mangan, *Athleticism*, pp. 23 and 28.

[60]   Geoffrey Best, 'Militarism in the Victorian Public School' in *The Victorian Public School: Studies in the Development of an Educational Institution ed. by Brian Simon and Ian Bradley* (Dublin: Gill and Macmillan, 1975) pp. 129-146 (p.134).

[61]   Richard Osborne, *Music & Musicians of Eton* (London: The Cygnet Press, 2012), pp. 53-63.

[62]   Michael Meredith, *Five Hundred Years of Eton Theatre* (Eton, Eton College, 2001), pp. 15-16.

Chapter 4.

2.7 Conclusion

The landscape of Eton changed considerably over the course of the Victorian period, in a way which reflected broader trends. Far from being a fortress of conservatism against the tides of modernity, Eton was swept along with the rest of the country. A number of Victorian trends – the railways, domesticity, closer supervision of children, professionalisation, secularisation – have been shown to have affected the fabric and working practices of Eton. Furthermore, accounts of this period are often dominated by the Clarendon Commission of 1861-1864, yet a number of the changes mentioned predate it. It can thus be seen that even if one removes the Clarendon Commission from consideration, Eton can still be said to have been subject to the border forces affecting English society.

3. People: Victorian Eton as a Community

Having analysed Victorian Eton as a changing space, this study will now consider the people within it. Again, the method will be comparative, focusing on the differences between the start and end of the Victorian period. It will be seen that the size of the school community expanded considerably. Furthermore, people's roles and daily lives changed in significant ways. These developments, it will be argued, reflect the broader trends that were affecting English society as a whole.

3.1 Eton Parents

The role of the people who sent their boys to Eton can be analysed from two angles: families' relationships with boys while they were at Eton; and families' dealings with Eton and its staff. There was broad continuity in the former, reinforcing family historians' views that very little changed. However, a great change can be noticed in the latter. This indicates that, even as parents' direct relationships with their Etonian sons changed little over the Victorian period, their indirect relationship with them through their sons' school changed considerably, causing the school to change in its turn.

Fletcher, French and Rothery find very little change in what wealthy parents and their sons wrote to each other about over the course of the Victorian period.[63] Central to this is the idea of the 'complacent family' as expressed by Honey, and also elaborated by Chandos and Mangan, whereby parents went along with the deprivations inflicted by the boarding school experience on their boys because of the advantages to be gained.[64] For Eton, these views are supported by

---

[63]   Fletcher, *Growing up in England*, p. 207; French and Rothery, p. 78.

[64]   Fletcher, *Growing up in England*, p. 196; Honey, p. 203; Chandos, pp. 66-70; Mangan, *Athleticism*, p. 129.

primary evidence spanning the whole period. For example, the letters of Edward Herbert (at Eton 1851-55) deal principally with routine matters, such as arrival, departure and food.[65] The letters of three generations of the Spicer family (attending Eton at various points between 1831 and 1904) are in a similar vein.[66] It can be noted that parents' letters were broadly in sympathy with the values of school. Mothers as well as fathers participated in the ongoing formation of male gender roles by emphasising those character traits which would assure their sons' progress through school and success in life.[67] For example, in a letter of 1853, Edward Herbert is advised to avoid taking up modern languages, lest this harm his progress in his main school work.[68] At the other end of the period, Edward Christie-Miller (at Eton 1894-98) is eager to show his parents that he is doing well.[69]

---

[65] ECA, ED 383.

[66] ECA, ED 351.

[67] French and Rothery, p. 35.

[68] ECA, ED 383 01 36.

[69] ECA, ED 67 04 01-24.

Although analysis of letters between boys and their families presents a picture of continuity, the limits of letters as evidence must be noted. Some boys received more letters than others, and perhaps those of modest means who potentially had most to complain of would not have been able to afford to send as many letters and, if they did, their families may not have been among those who had the storage space or public status to feel it worth keeping family records for posterity. Moreover, in all the letters studied, as boys mature, their tone becomes more controlled and it becomes clear that, as they grow up, they are also growing apart from their families. From other sources, such as the *Eton College Chronicle* or administrative documents, it is apparent that there was a whole world of activities in which the boys could immerse themselves. If the boys chose not to share much of this with their parents, focusing instead on routine matters and maintaining ties of affection, then it is no surprise that focusing on letters as a source leads to the conclusion that very little changed. Through being selective about the content of their letters, the boys were learning the ability to balance the demands of the 'two worlds' of the public sphere and the private sphere.[70] Therefore, is necessary to look beyond letters if one wants to develop a full picture of the boys' lives at school.

With regard to parents' relationship with the school, a major change is to be observed over the course of the Victorian period. At the beginning of the period, the dominant tone can be said to be aristocratic hauteur, with the paterfamilias remaining aloof from the hired underlings to whom he had delegated various functions, including his sons' education.[71] By the end of the period, a rather more middle class approach can be discerned, whereby the boys' education was seen as an investment to be monitored rather than simply a function to be delegated. This is apparent in head masters' communications with parents. Hawtrey's letters are brief, almost apologising for having to enter into communication at all.[72] Warre's letters are longer and it is clear that he expects his readers to want to hear

---

[70]   French and Rothery, p. 82.

[71]   Roberts, p. 68-9.

[72]   ECA, COLL/P13.

full details.[73] Doubtless Warre was helped by technology (many of his letters are typed) and improvements in the transport and postal systems. But implicit in these same advances was an expectation of greater professionalism.

The movement to reform Eton is further evidence of parents' relations with Eton (and, indirectly, with their Etonian sons), and suggests that much changed in the culture surrounding the school. Calls for reform had been published in the press from 1810 onwards. They were principally made by former pupils.[74] If they were not parents of boys at the school at the time of writing, they wrote from the perspective of those members of the upper middle classes who complained of 'a poor investment with little return for the capital outlay'.[75] Leading the charge was 'Paterfamilias', a pen name chosen to indicate a 'sensible, concerned parent', author of a series of closely argued letters to the *Cornhill*

---

[73] ECA, COLL/P05.

[74] Mack, vol. II, pp. 8-13.

[75] Peter Parker, *The Old Lie: The Great War and the public-school ethos* (London: Constable, 1987), p. 40.

Magazine.[76] This movement did not make much impact at the start of the Victorian period; by the end, its proposals for reform of the curriculum and accommodation had been acted upon, with Warre keeping his own heavily annotated company of the commission's report.[77] The key difference was that, by the 1860s, the portion of the middle classes who sent their sons to public schools were 'firmly in the saddle' in an England enjoying peace and unprecedented prosperity.[78] The influence they had acquired by the middle of the Victorian period explains the intensity of the campaign at that time and also its success in forcing a parliamentary commission of inquiry.

It can thus be seen that, over the course of the Victorian period, an increasing number of parents, even at this most aristocratic of schools, were not content to maintain an aristocratic aloofness with regard to the functioning of Eton. It was not sufficient that their boys be able to socialise with the

[76]   Ibid., p. 40; Mack, vol. II, p. 8.

[77]   ECA, COLL/P05.

[78]   Mack, vol. II, p. 4.

sons of the rich and powerful. By the 1860s, a very middle class concern about value for money held sway for a sufficient proportion of those who sent or would send their sons to Eton. The Victorian phenomenon of public examinations played an important part.[79] It was no good paying fees for Eton and then also having to send your son to a crammer afterwards in order for him to pass the examinations set by the universities or the army.[80] This was as much the case among many of the aristocracy as it was among the wealthier elements of the middle classes, as the decline in agriculture and emergence of new professions meant that the sons of even the most established families would need to compete with others for university places and jobs.[81] In a large and traditional institution like Eton, change could only take place as a consequence of changes among the

---

[79]   French and Rothery, p. 239.

[80]   Parker, p. 42.

[81]   John Mogey, 'Review of *Victorian Values: Secularism and the Size of Families* by J. A. Banks', *Journal of Marriage and Family*, 44.3 (1982), pp. 812-813; Simon R. S. Szreter , 'Review of *Victorian Values: Secularism and the Size of Families* by J. A. Banks', *The Historical Journal*, 26.1 (Mar. , 1983), pp. 257-259; Leslie Page Moch, 'Review of *Victorian Values: Secularism and the Size of Families* by J. A. Banks', *Journal of Social History*, 17.2 (Winter, 1983), pp. 355-357.

groups who sent their sons to be educated there. The campaign to reform Eton can thus be seen as a reflection of broader socio-economic changes having an effect on parents and their expectations of the school, and then on the school itself.

3.2 Eton Boys

The number of boys at Eton almost doubled over the course of the Victorian period.[82] This is part of the broader phenomenon of the rise of the middle classes amidst the peace and unprecedented prosperity that England enjoyed over the course of the nineteenth century, and their demand for a prestigious education for their children, resulting in the opening of several new public schools from the 1840s onwards and high numbers for the more established schools.[83] This was facilitated by the railway revolution, which allowed families throughout the country and, indeed, the empire, to consider Eton

---

[82]   See Appendix B: Pupil Population at Eton 1820-1910.

[83]   Gathorne-Hardy, pp. 105-113.

as logistically feasible.[84]

Regarding boys' background, the sources considered provide details of a boy's family if it conforms to contemporary notions of distinction, principally if the father has some kind of noble, clerical or military title. Boys for whom information is not supplied may well have belonged to families of more modest rank, but the wide-ranging research required to investigate this is beyond the scope of this study. However, the evidence to hand confirms the established view that, on the one hand, Eton had a more aristocratic pupil population than any other school, while, at the same time, it was incorporating a growing number of boys from rising middle class families, along with a middle class culture that encouraged all Eton families to expect a more professional service in return for the high fees paid.[85]

As regards the boys' lives, the change from an entirely classical to a more modern curriculum has been analysed in Chapter 2. A consideration of

---

[84]   Bamford, p. 59.

[85]   Mack, vol. II, p. 121.

memoirs indicates that the experiences that stood out in later years were the things boys did outside the schoolroom.[86] At the start of the Victorian period, boys' lives at Eton were defined by the 'liberties'.[87] This was the de facto practice of leaving the boys to govern themselves, the result of a traditional attitude that what happened beyond the schoolroom was not the masters' concern. This laissez-faire approach had given rise to a whole boy-run world, in which boys could theoretically do what they wished, although it also resulted in the domination of the weak by the strong, including such customs as fagging. [88] The 'liberties' were a key part of the boys' educational experience, with the (aristocratic) boys' defiance against the (middle class) masters becoming a process

---

[86]   Howard Warburton Elphinstone, *Recollections of the Thirties and Forties of the Nineteenth Century* (For Private Circulation: nd); Arthur Coleridge, *Eton in the Forties* (London: Richard Bentley and Son, 1896); A. G. L'Estrange, *Vert de Vert's Eton Days* (London: Elliot Stock, 1887); W. C. Green, *Memories of Eton and King's* (Eton: Spottiswoode & Co., 1905); Arthur Campbell Ainger, *Memories of Eton Sixty Ago* (London: John Murray, 1917); E. Parker, *Eton in the 'Eighties* (London: Macmillan, 1914); C. H. Marten, *Recollections of an Eton Colleger, 1898-1902* (Eton: Spottiswoode and Co., 1905).

[87]   Chandos, pp. 110-132.

[88]   Ibid., pp. 86-87.

of 'trial and growth.'[89] Attempts by the school authorities to rein in boy behaviour had resulted in three major rebellions since the time of the French Revolution, which in turn explain the harsh measures taken by John Keate, Hawtrey's predecessor.[90]

By the end of the Victorian period, boys' lives at Eton were defined by games.

Tosh finds that the Victorian middle classes devised an 'intrusive and burdensome régime' for their children and, by the late nineteenth century, this had found its way to Eton.[91] In addition to a broader curriculum and increased workload, there was greater supervision through an entirely school-run boarding house system.[92] But the school-wide system of games was the major feature of this régime. A contemporary account explains how far games had taken over Etonians' lives since the start of the Victorian period:

---

[89]   Ibid., p. 167.

[90]   Ibid., pp. 175-184.

[91]   Tosh, 'Domesticity and Manliness in the Victorian Middle Class', p. 60.

[92]   Byrne and Churchill, pp. 37-39 and 130.

And now there are fifty fives courts where before there was one; twenty games or thereabouts of cricket as against three; compulsory football for every house four or five times a week; to say nothing of beagles and athletic sports in the Easter Term, and rowing and bathing daily through the summer...[93]

Some did resist, as expressed through a letter to *The Times* (20 September 1899) denouncing the 'new tyranny' of compulsory football.[94] However, judging by the prominence of sporting achievements in a range of Old Etonian obituaries, it is evident that games had occupied not just the time and energies of Etonians, but also their imaginations many years on.[95] The contrast with the unruliness of the boys on the eve of the Victorian period makes plain the value of

---

[93]   Lionel Ford, 'Public School Athletics' in *Chapters on Secondary Education* ed. by Christopher Cookson (1898) (Reprint, London: Forgotten Books, 2013), pp. 290-91.

[94]   Mack, vol. II, p. 210.

[95]   ECA, ED 354 57.

games as a method of social control, enabling the Eton authorities to accommodate a larger than ever population of boys while running the school in an increasingly efficient manner.[96] The boys' leisure activities were a form of conspicuous consumption which the school took over for its own professional purposes, indicating that the school's aristocratic culture was being suffused with bourgeois values.

3.3 Eton Masters

In 1849, when Edmond Warre (head master at the end of the Victorian period) arrived as a boy in Hawtrey's Eton, there were sixteen classical masters and three mathematical masters as well as a few 'extra masters' for French, German, Italian, drawing, dancing and fencing. Games were far less organised and masters took no part in them at all. By 1899, the number of masters had increased to forty. The Mathematical masters had by now been incorporated into the main body of teaching staff as fully-fledged masters.

---

[96] Mangan, *Athleticism*, p. 68.

At the start of the Victorian period, masters had no responsibilities beyond the schoolroom but boys were theoretically not allowed outside the school precincts. This resulted in the institutionalised hypocrisy of 'shirking': boys could go to the river or the shops as long as no master saw them; if one was walking past, the boy had to hide.[97] In the 1890s, masters had taken on a range of other duties beyond the schoolroom. Indeed, by this time, as Warre said in a circular to his colleagues, 'a master is never truly off duty'.[98] They were running boarding houses and, in a remarkable development, were now taking an active part in games. As Mangan observes, the archetypal master had by now changed from 'dry pedant' to 'perpetual schoolboy'.[99]

A number of the trends operating in Victorian society can be observed in the changes that took place in the composition and functions of the teaching staff. Firstly, one can observe the phenomenon of

---

[97]   *Guide to Eton: Eton Alphabet; Eton Block; Eton Glossary* (London: Whittaker and Co. , 1861), p. 33.

[98]   ECA, COLL/P05.

[99]   Mangan, *Athleticism*, p. 113.

secularisation, with fewer staff in holy orders. In 1840, all fifteen masters were in holy orders; by 1899, this was down to thirteen out of forty.[100] In the 1850s, Bamford notes that there took place a significant appointment of lay masters in public schools, indicating a broad change in approach: the care of the boys' souls had given way to the care of their minds and bodies. For 1893, Bamford counts 47 lay masters in Eton, compared to 10 who were clerics, a development that was mirrored in other schools.[101]

Concomitant with this is the phenomenon of professionalization, which is a discernible phenomenon in a number of areas of British society by the end of the nineteenth century.[102] Whereas in the preindustrial social system, wealth had been principally associated with land and capital, the last two decades of the nineteenth century had seen the rise, in terms of importance and numbers, of professions whose chief labour consisted in offering

---

[100]   See Appendix D: masters 1840-50 and Appendix E: masters 1890-1900.

[101]   Bamford, p. 56.

[102]   Perkin; also J. F. C. Harrison, *Late Victorian Britain* (London: Routledge, 2013).

specific knowledge and skills.[103]   Professionalisation
was becoming prevalent in the world of science and
scholarship and, among schoolmasters, the
expectation that a man teaching at a public school be
in holy orders had diminished with the growing
recognition that schoolmastering itself was a
profession.[104]

3.4 Eton Women

The boys spent most of their time outside the
schoolroom. Therefore, it is important to consider the
non-teaching staff, especially staff associated with
boarding houses. This offers an opportunity to test
another widely asserted notion, which is the idea that
the boarding school was a male-only environment to
which boys were sent to develop away from the
feminising influence home. With the rise of
domesticity, the home was becoming a female-

---

[103]   Perkin, p. xii.

[104]   Robert Anderson, 'Learning: Education, class and culture' in
The Victorian World (London: Routledge, 2012) ed. by Martin
Hewitt, pp. 484-5; also Elizabeth Gargano, *Reading Victorian
Schoolrooms* (London: Routledge, 2008), p. 78.

dominated space.[105] It therefore became all the more important for the paterfamilias to send his sons away in order to acquire the skills and knowledge required to function and flourish in the homosocial environments (such as politics, commerce, the military and the church) where they would have to make a living. Tosh argues that, in the 'all-male' atmosphere of public schools, women were 'effectively banished as points of emotional reference', so that 'freed of female distraction, the schools could get on with their real job of installing manliness'.[106] Gathorne-Hardy posits an anthropological understanding of this practice, linking it with the rite of passage known as 'extrusion', whereby children are removed from the family environment in order to be forced to acquire survival skills for adult life, as well as developing bonds of loyalty to a wider community that goes beyond the nuclear family.[107]

However, an analysis of the census shows that a

---

[105]   Tosh, *A Man's Place*, pp. 117-118.

[106]   Ibid.; also Roberts, p. 68.

[107]   Gathorne-Hardy, pp. 469-75.

large number of women were resident in Eton. In some buildings, the male to female ratio is equal.[108] This indicates that Eton was not a purely homosocial milieu. An analysis of gender dynamics within Eton would therefore correspond to the call by historians of masculinity for men's identities to be studied in relation to those of women (rather than simply focusing on homosocial environments).[109]

A useful analytical tool here is R. W. Connell's concept of hegemonic masculinity, especially if one incorporates the added distinction between external and internal hegemony. Hegemonic masculinity is a normative pattern of practice which 'embodied the currently most honored way of being a man [...]'. It '[...] required all other men to position themselves in relation to it, and it ideologically legitimated the global

---

[108]   1851 England Census, Buckinghamshire, Parish of Eton, Enumeration District 6c (PRO HO 107/1718), pp. 1-36; 1851 England Census, Buckinghamshire, Parish of Eton, Enumeration District 6d (PRO HO 107/1718), pp. 1-25; 1891 England Census, Buckinghamshire, Parish of Eton, Enumeration District 5 (PRO RG 12/1134), pp. 1-19. (Digital images from Ancestry.com <http://www.ancestry.com> [accessed 12 July 2014].)

[109]   Francis, p. 652.

subordination of women to men.'[110] Those men who
were able to act fully in accordance with this pattern
of practice achieved dominance in society. For those
men who did not, and for women, the most
straightforward way to find some measure of power
and security was to support and act in accordance
with the dominant pattern of practice.[111] External
hegemony refers to the power exercised by men,
especially dominant men, over women; internal
hegemony is the hierarchy of dominance among men,
with those closer to 'the currently most honored way
of being a man' exercising power over others.[112]

Looking at a range of primary sources, it
becomes apparent how being at Eton could be an
apprenticeship in internal and external hegemony. It
is already clear, especially from memoirs, that boys
had to navigate an internal hierarchy of power
dynamics, with fags at one end, captains of houses

---

[110] R. W. Connell and J. W. Messerschmidt, 'Hegemoic
Masculinity Rethinking the Concept', *Gender and Society*, 19:6
(2005), 833.
[111] French and Rothery, p. 5.
[112] Ibid.

and games at the other.[113] The census shows us that Eton was far from a male-only environment, but that the majority of females whom the boys lived alongside occupied subservient positions. Their dealings with these maids and serving girls was an education in productively coexisting with their inferiors, gaining from the unequal power dynamic but also conducting oneself in such a way as to leave the other person happy to be of service.

Not all females in Eton were in a position of subservience, but it can still be discerned how the boys were imbibing the workings of internal and external hegemony. In a memoir published in 1905 by a retired master who himself had been the son of a master and had grown up in Eton in the 1830s and 1840s, the author mentions fond memories of games with the daughter of a colleague of his father. But he goes on to make clear that such mixed activities could happen only in enclosed spaces, such as a private garden; outdoor play in public spaces could involve

---

[113]   Chandos, pp. 86-109.

only boys.[114] He was thus socialised into the boundaries of hegemonic masculinity. As for women who occupied positions of some seniority, the boys' and their male elders' dealings with them demonstrated the limits of this seniority, as will be made clear in the next few paragraphs. Roper and Tosh put it as follows:

> [... While] women played a central role as workers and 'stand-in' mothers, their activities were continually dismissed as peripheral. While mummy, matron and the maids serviced the boys' physical and emotional needs, the achievement of manhood depended on a disparagement of the feminine without and within.[115]

Being sent away to Eton – the *rite de passage* of extrusion, as Gathorne-Hardy calls it – was therefore not simply to toughen boys up away from the

---

[114] Green, *Memories of Eton and King's* (1905), p. 11 and p. 16.

[115] Roper and Tosh, *Manful Assertions*, p. 13.

feminising influences of home. And it was not just to socialise them into functioning within the homosocial milieus where they were to spend their working lives. Rather, a boy's attendance of Eton during the Victorian period – regardless of the family's motives – can be understood as an apprenticeship in male privilege, through which he learnt to navigate the paths of internal and external hegemonic masculinity.

3.5 Dames and House Masters

More women occupy the most senior positions within boarding houses in the 1840s than in the 1890s. At the start of the Victorian period, the boarding houses were mostly run by local landladies. The official title was dame and even a man who ran a boarding house was called a dame (or sometimes a dominie). These enterprising women were given the respect and status thought befitting someone who superintended the living arrangements of the sons of gentlemen and noblemen. This respect often turned into objectification, as was often the case when men tried to deal with women in positions of seniority.

Accounts of nineteenth-century boarding house dames often fall into the language of objectification. Sophia Florella Angelo, daughter of the fencing master and head of Angelo's boarding house from 1810 to 1847, was referred to as 'a noted beauty' or 'a pretty brunette educated abroad', and was styled 'the Duchess of Eton'.[116] Another dame at the start of the Victorian period, Mrs Drury, is described by H. E. Luxmoore, a famous turn-of-the-century Eton master, in language that draws from a similar vein:

> I as a small boy used to meet Mrs Drury (and admire her) at my Uncle's, the Rev. C. Luxmoore's. She was very prepossessing and pleasant and was liked by her boys.[117]

This objectifying language reaches a height in some verses, published in Bernard Blackmantle's *The English Spy* in 1825. Although this was just over a

---

[116]   'Notes on the Eton dames of the Nineteenth Century', *Etoniana,* 34 (31 July 1923), p. 529.

[117]   'Notes on the Eton dames of the Nineteenth Century', *Etoniana,* 34 (31 July 1923), p. 532.

decade before the start of the Victorian period, the set-up described and the sensibility evoked were part of the Eton of the 1840s and had all but disappeared by the end of the 1890s. Under the title 'The dames of Eton are being summoned by Mercury before the Muse', the verses treat the Eton dame as goddesses, singing the praises of each one. There were men, some of them masters, also keeping boarding houses at this time, but the verses single out the women for this treatment:

> A crowd pressing forward, the day growing late,
>
> Truth whisper'd the Muse, "we had better retreat;
>
> For though 'mong the dames we are free from disasters,
>
> I know not how well we may fare with the masters.
>
> There's Carter, and Yonge, Knapp, Green and Dupuis,
>
> All coming this way with their ladies, I see.
>
> Our visit, you know, was alone to the belles;
>
> The masters may sing, if they please, of themselves."[118]

---

[118] 'Eton dames in 1825', *Etoniana,* 3 (30 November 1904), p. 46.

The editors of *The English Spy* explain to their readers that Carter, Yonge, Knapp, Green and Dupuis were masters who kept boarding houses, noting that this was a practice which had only recently become permitted but which, 'it must be confessed' was proving to be:

> a salutary arrangement, as it not only tends to keep the youth in a better state of subjection, but in many instances is calculated to increase their progress in study, by enabling them to receive private instruction.[119]

The special status of dames meant prestige and praise but no official authority. There are several reports which indicate that the dames had no authority to discipline boys and had to call upon masters for help when the boys' behaviour was out of hand. There is a story of Sophia Angelo, being 'broziered' by her boys. Broziering was a prank

---

[119]   'Eton dames in 1825', *Etoniana,* 3 (30 November 1904), p. 46.

whereby boys would conspire, at a meal time, to keep asking for food until the dame had entirely run out. The dame could not simply refuse, for fear of loss of face. Thus for all the food to be eaten until she had no more to offer was a crushing humiliation for the dame and a triumph for the boys. On being broziered, Miss Angelo is said to have complained to a master, who contrived to set the offending boys work so difficult that they were unable to complete it, which then gave him the pretext for having them thrashed.[120] However uncommon such an occurrence was, and however embellished the story became, this neatly evokes the culture of the time, in which the dame, though respected and praised, did not have the authority to either refuse unreasonable requests or punish bad behaviour and, moreover, could not be seen to be the direct cause for the boys being disciplined, thus causing the master to engineer a pretext for doing so. There are other, more routine examples. The Misses Evans, as conscientious as they were in their care for the boys in their house, still needed the intervention of masters when stiff

---

[120]   Ibid., p. 529.

discipline needed to be enforced or official measures needed to be taken.[121] H. E. Luxmoore mentions arriving as a novice master at Eton and lodging in the house run by Madame de Rosen, who regularly called upon him and other masters lodging with her to impose discipline. These masters were called 'house masters' in the sense that they lodged in a boys' boarding house and imposed discipline when the dame required them to do so. This could involve such tasks as taking a roll call, reprimanding boys or reporting their behaviour to the head master, all of which were, if not entirely impossible for dames, certainly considered more properly the province of masters.[122]

At the end of the Victorian period, a 'house master' had acquired an entirely different status and function. He was a member of the teaching staff who was also in charge of a boarding house and responsible for the overall welfare and education of the boys lodging with him. However, class distinction

---

[121]   E. Gambier-Parry, *Annals of an Eton House* (London: John Murray, 1907), p. 260.

[122]   'Notes on the Eton dames of the Nineteenth Century', p. 531.

of sorts remained, for those masters running a house who did not teach classics were still referred to as dames.[123]

Although running a boarding house could prove a welcome boost to a master's income, taking on what was regarded as women's work could undermine their status among colleagues and boys. A report from 1828 mentions Hawtrey's predecessor as head master, John Keate, receiving five complaints from Edward Dobson, a tutor who ran a boarding house, that boys were 'cutting him'. Keate took no notice, saying: 'He complained once for being called a Dominie [masculine for dame]; he begins to affect rather too much.'[124] By the middle of the Victorian period, the number of masters going into business running boarding houses had increased to the point where approximately half the boarding accommodation was run by dames and half was run by masters; there were many 'dames versus Tutors' sports fixtures, as such teams represented about half

---

[123]   Byrne, and Churchill, pp. 126-129.

[124]   'Notes on the Eton dames of the Nineteenth Century', p. 531.

of the boys each.[125] By the end of the nineteenth century, there was just one dame, Miss Evans, running a house, while all others were run by fully fledged masters. The school authorities had centralised residential arrangements, and had begun the process of purchasing all boarding houses.[126]

This development reflects two trends that had taken hold of Eton by the end of the Victorian period: middle class family values, with greater supervision of all aspects of children's lives; and professionalisation, with the school taking on this supervision as part of its responsibilities to its customers. Two further effects of professionalisation can be discerned. First, there is managerialism and bureaucracy. The allocation of a housemastership was now in the head master's gift, which had the effect of consolidating his powers and increasing his administrative workload, contributing to the transformation of his role from chief teacher to general manager. Second, professionalisation resulted

---

[125]   *Eton College Chronicle*, no. 1 (14 May 1863), pp. 2-3.

[126]   Bamford, p. 194; Byrne and Churchill, pp. 129-130.

in masculinisation, here as elsewhere in nineteenth-century English society when a particular field of work was reorganized and modernised. (An earlier example is medical care during childbirth.[127]) While Edward Dobson, running a boarding house in the 1820s, was mocked for being a 'dominie', his successors at the end of the nineteenth-century enjoyed officially bestowed respect and prestige because the school recognised that this was an important part of its provision and, moreover, because it was no longer associated with women's work.

Therefore, the emergence of the role of house master, with the status and functions that it had at the end of the Victorian period, can be understood as a reflection of the rise of middle class values in English society, whereby the close supervision of children was recognised as a task of vital importance. This was in a society that was at once deeply patriarchal and

---

[127]   Ornella Moscucci, *The science of woman: gynaecology and gender in England, 1800-1929.* (Cambridge: Cambridge University Press, 1993) p. 10; Ellen Jordan, 'The Exclusion of Women from Industry in Nineteenth-Century Britain', *Comparative Studies in Society and History*, Vol. 31, No. 2 (Apr., 1989), pp. 273-296.

increasingly professionalized, with the consequence that this vital task was taken on by men with an official status within the institution, and for whom it was recognised that this task was one of their key responsibilities.

3.6 Conclusion

This chapter and the previous chapter form a response to two tendencies in historians' treatments of Victorian public schools: studies approaching them from the perspective of the history of the family tend to treat them as unchanging; accounts of the Victorian age in school histories often focus on certain developments, such as the cult of games or the Clarendon Commission, to the exclusion of a range of changes that took place throughout the period as a result of broader social trends (listed in the Introduction). The previous chapter's analysis of changes to Eton as a space, together with this chapter's analysis of changes among people and practices within that space, has demonstrated the breadth of the changes undergone by the school and its community over the Victorian period.

These developments need to be distinguished from the various discourses that surrounded them. When analysing school communities, it is all the more important for the historian to be wary of conflating realities and rhetoric. Schools are by definition prescriptive institutions which aim to affirm and celebrate particular norms.[128] Now that these surface realities have been identified and discussed, it will be possible to move onto an analysis of the surrounding discourses. The analysis of Eton as a space and of the community which occupied that space will serve as context for an analysis of the values of the community, which will be the focus of the next chapter.

---

[128]   Mangan, *Athleticism*, p. xxx.

4. Values: The *Eton College Chronicle* as a source for the ethos of Victorian Eton

4.1 Introduction

The research for this chapter used the *Eton College Chronicle* as a source for the values of the community to which an increasing number of late-Victorian families aspired to send their sons.[129] It focused on issues from Eton under Edmond Warre (head master 1884-1905), including a comparative analysis of issues from the start and towards the end of his tenure. This is a different approach to the previous two chapters, which compared Eton at the start and end of the Victorian period. As the *Chronicle* started in 1863, using that approach would have

---

[129]   See Appendix B. Also: Ogilvie, pp. 139-179; Honey, *Tom Brown's Universe*, ch. 4.

required comparing different types of source. This is a source-intensive analysis and consistency in material is required. Warre's tenure was chosen as, by 1884, the *Chronicle* had developed the format which it would continue to have until the mid-twentieth century. Moreover, it will become apparent that, even within these two decades, considerable change in the culture of the school can be discerned. For the sake of broader context, earlier and later issues of the *Chronicle* were also analysed.

4.2 School periodicals as a source

Mangan has conducted such an analysis of six other schools and makes some observations on the school magazine as a primary source. He points out its 'introspective' role, and its use in revealing the priorities and values of a close-knit community.[130] Mangan also highlights the role of censorship: however much various contributors sought to challenge established values, censorship by the authorities meant that the magazine was always more

---

[130]   Mangan, *Athleticism*,

likely to perpetuate such values. There are a number
of ephemeral publications which challenge the
dominant culture, and the study of these can reveal
much about views of a minority of boys as well as
providing a useful source for Victorian adolescence.[131]
Yet the effects of censorship and the *Chronicle*'s status
as an official record make it all the more useful for
the purposes of discovering the dominant values of
the community. Mangan also underlines the role of
the boy editors. These were likely to have been boys
more inclined to intellectual and literary pursuits and
Mangan mentions a broad trend whereby the editors'
inclinations to print scholarly and creative content
were counterbalanced by the popular demand for
coverage of sport, citing examples from other
schools.[132] Finally, Mangan emphasizes the use of the
biographical material often published in school
magazines as evidence for the priorities and values of

---

[131]   Jenny Holt, 'The Textual Formations of Adolescence in Turn-
of-the-Century Youth Periodicals: The "Boy's Own Paper" and Eton
College Ephemeral Magazines', *Victorian Periodicals Review*, Vol.
35, No. 1 (Spring, 2002), pp. 63-88.

[132]   Mangan, *Athleticism*, Appendix III (a), also chapters 4 and 5.

the community.[133]

4.3 Method

The case study in this chapter involved four stages. First, issues from 1884 to 1898 were scrutinized to develop a clear idea of style and key themes. Second, any allusions to family and home life were noted. Third, and in order to provide a corrective to any possibility of confirmation bias in the first two stages, a comparative analysis was undertaken of issues from October 1884 and October 1898 in order to build up a statistical picture of how the dominant values of the community may have changed within this period. This involved investigating the relative emphasis given to values which scholarship on the Victorian family has mentioned as competing for influence during this period: athleticism; militarism (including empire); aestheticism and intellectualism (considered together); domesticity and religion.[134] It also involved

---

[133]   Ibid.

[134]   John Tosh, *A man's place: Masculinity and the middle-class*

comparative analysis of an element particular to the history of public schools and which has special relevance to the study of developments in the care of boys: the 'liberties', discussed in the section on boys in Chapter 3. Fourth, a study of earlier and later issues provided further context.

4.4 Analysis

The first stage of the analysis revealed that sport dominated each issue, often receiving the first mention in the editorial and then filling the majority of the first few pages. There is often an explicit link drawn between sport and masculinity such as a report of an Old Etonian dinner in which the chairman praises the 'value of the discipline of all manly games'.[135] The context was a speech about an Eton

---

home in Victorian England (New Haven and London: Yale University Press, 1999); Martin Francis, 'The domestication of the male? Recent research on nineteenth-and twentieth-century British masculinity', *The Historical Journal* 45.3 (2002): 637-652; Leonore Davidoff and Catherine Hall, *Family Fortunes* (Oxford: Routledge, 2002); Lesley A. Hall, *Sex, Gender and Social Change in Britain since 1880* (Basingstoke: Palgrave, 2013).

[135]   *Eton College Chronicle (ECC)*, no. 809, p. 547.

charity working with young men in a deprived part of London, further underlining the importance of athleticism as a value which the Eton community did not simply want to promote within itself, but also share with others. Sporting prowess is not praised without qualification; there is frequent mention of an underpinning morality. One editorial criticizes 'placing oneself before one's side'.[136]

After sport, the area of Eton life which seems to receive the greatest coverage is the Eton College Rifle Volunteers, with shooting matches and field days covered in great depth. There are also many other references to militaristic values, such as obituaries of Old Etonians who died defending the empire. Indeed, it is striking how often sport, militarism and empire are celebrated together. A letter reporting a gathering of Old Etonian officers in Egypt jokes that the large number of oarsmen amongst them has been 'of the greatest service in the Nile Expedition'.[137] A write-up of a ceremony on the

---

[136]   *ECC*, no. 387, p. 1547.
[137]   *ECC*, no. 397, p. 1590.

retirement of R. A. H. Mitchell, the master who coached the cricket XI, mentions that every single captain of cricket from 1866 to 1897 had gathered, noting and dwelling poignantly on the one exception, the captain in 1872, who was killed in the Zulu war 'like a good cricketer and good Englishman giving his life for his side'. [138]

Sport dominated, and militarism and empire were celebrated, but intellectualism and aestheticism had a place. Certain items can, in line with Mangan's observations, likely be attributed to a minority tendency within the school given voice by boy editors with literary inclinations, such as an editorial decrying the time wasted on sport and the decline in reading.[139] There are other items which suggest that intellectualism was respected within the school community as a whole. One example is the frequent listing of winners of academic prizes. However, it is worth nothing that these are listed in a similar fashion to sporting accolades and thus can be said to form

---

[138]   *ECC*, no. 807, p. 540

[139]   *ECC*, no. 377, p. 1507.

part of a broader competitive spirit within Eton, which one could venture was initially and principally nourished by games. Notices bidding welcome or farewell to masters celebrate that individual's achievements, be they scholarly or sporting or both. Furthermore, it is surprising to note a certain amount of coverage given to music and literary discussions. While it is evident that such activities did not enjoy the widespread popularity and participation of sport, it can be observed that this was a community in which those who were not athletically inclined could pursue other interests. Indeed, one such area of school life was writing and editing the *Chronicle* itself. However, sport does dominate and it is evident that the editors recognized its primacy ('The first thing that claims attention this half is naturally football'), whatever their personal interests.

At this point, it became necessary to consider the authorship of the source. There are no by-lines, but there is no reason to consider the *Chronicle* to be a deviation from the practice set out by Mangan, whereby boys would compile the magazine, mostly consisting of other boys' work, and then submit it for the approval of the school authorities. Its content indicates that this was a community in which the older boys still had considerable power, albeit now accompanied by greater responsibility and always under at least nominal supervision by masters. This is evident in the reports on sports matches in which one mention may be made of the house master and, rarer still, the coach, but then the burden of decision-making, selection and leadership evidently falls on the senior boys involved. This is also the case in other activities, such as the Literary Society and the Debating Society. This was the organizational culture which the school sought to promote for itself and it would be sensible to deduce that the production of the *Chronicle* worked along the same lines. Of course, in practice there were bound to be tensions between the 'liberties' of old and the increasing involvement by masters in spheres of school life beyond the schoolroom, which is occasionally mentioned in letters to the *Chronicle*.[140]

The second stage involved identifying any mentions of home or family life. It is necessary to

---

[140]   *ECC*, no. 380, p. 1519.

take into account the genre, authorship, audience and milieu of the source. This is the magazine of a boys' school, written by boys, mostly for other Etonians (present or former) and all of this in a strongly patriarchal society. Coverage of domesticity will be rare but all the more useful for revealing tensions with the masculinity which the Eton community sought to uphold. There is a passing reference to such tension in the issue dedicated to the Eton versus Harrow cricket match which contains a complaint about the admittance of ladies to the Eton stand at Lord's and the consequent obstruction of the view as 'every lady wears a huge hat with feathers, &c'.[141] While the writer of the complaint attempts to maintain a practical tone, this is evocative of other objections to female encroachment on a male space, such as in debates over women's participation in church.[142] There is a discernible revulsion at the presence of femininity in a space which is not just male-dominated but is intended to celebrate virility.

---

[141] *ECC*, no. 809, p. 545.

[142] Davidoff and Hall, p. 131.

An even more remarkable example can be found in the report on the presentation of the leaving portrait of Miss Evans, who ran the last of the dames' houses. It says that 'the proceedings throughout were of a strictly friendly and intimate nature', but is reluctant to go into further detail: 'there seems nothing to tell of them, and even that little appears almost like a violation of the sanctity of private life'.[143] This coyness makes evident the norm from which such proceedings were a departure: a more formal and regimented ethos that was the antithesis of the domestic milieu from which boys were being sent away in the first place, and of which this event was reminiscent. Miss Evans herself is emblematic of a shift taking place within Eton. Boarding houses, with the exception of hers, had been taken over by masters, reflecting the need perceived by the school authorities to take responsibility for all aspects of the boys' lives. Yet this move to greater professionalization involved an implicit masculinisation and a retreat from domesticity.[144]

---

[143]   *ECC*, no. 810, p. 552.

[144]   See also Chapter 2, dames and Maids.

The third stage of the source analysis involved a statistical comparison of the first three issues of the academic year in 1884 and 1898.[145] The value of athleticism predominates throughout.[146] It should be noted that, in 1898, the *Chronicle* had become weekly, and yet still found as much sport to cover as in 1884. There is a growth in reports that cover military matters and a decline in reports on intellectual and creative pursuits[147]. The theme of militarism also includes the idea of empire, as almost all mentions of the British Empire in the *Chronicle* address it from a military perspective, usually Old Etonians fighting and dying for the empire. It is possible to discern from this trend a growing emphasis on a masculinity that involves doing ones duty on the sports field and the battlefield, which can understood in the context of a ruling class that wanted its young men to do their best in the service of the empire.[148]

---

[145]   See Appendix F.

[146]   Ibid., Table 1.

[147]   Ibid.

[148]   Chandos, p. 344.

Religion, on the other hand, receives only occasional attention.[149] As for home life, there are two letters (one, curiously, for each year being compared) which purport to be from fathers of new boys, saying that they have just discovered that their little sons are obliged to play sport and complaining about the roughness of older boys. The tone suggests that these are jokes written by boys but, even if they are genuine, it is worth noting that the editors feel entitled to append some rather dismissive comments of their own. While home and church may have some claim on the boys' affections and beliefs, it is nowhere near as compelling as athleticism, militarism and empire. Alongside this, it is possible to detect a growing sense of fraternity built around these values. In the three 1898 issues, there was recurrent correspondence about the need for an Old Etonian colour, 'with the object of providing a means of recognition for Old Etonians in the colonies.'[150] This indicates a community in which boys are being encouraged to look away from home and family, and

---

[149]   See Appendix, Table 1.

[150]   *ECC*, no. 810, p. 552.

develop bonds with each other – bonds formed
playing for the house and the school, which will
endure while working and fighting for the empire.

A comparison was also made of the number
of articles which mention older boys taking charge of
school activities (in the spirit of the traditional
'liberties') against the number of articles which
showcase the involvement of masters.[151]

While a tension between the old order of boy liberties
and the new order of professional schoolmasters can
occasionally be detected in some of the articles
studied during the first stage of the analysis, the
statistical comparison does not indicate a marked
tendency in either direction. It could be tentatively
concluded that the two orders are receiving
approximately equal coverage, even as the
administration of Warre is bringing more and more
areas of school life under the control of masters.[152]
This indicates that, even as the 'liberties' are being
eroded in practice, the school community feels the

---

[151]   See Appendix, Table 2.

[152]   ECA, COLL P/05.

idea of boy power is worth continued emphasis. Again, this can be understood in the context of a ruling elite eager for their sons to have an apprenticeship in leadership.[153]

4.5 Further context

Scrutiny of the very first issues of the *Chronicle* in 1863 reveals that games enjoyed the same prominence as at the end of the nineteenth century, with a similar ratio between coverage of athletic and intellectual/creative matters. Domesticity receives similarly short shrift, even if there are, at this stage, enough dames running houses for there to be a regular sports fixture between a team representing all houses under the supervision of dames and a team representing all houses under the supervision of masters. However, there are more reports on events in the Chapel and no references to the empire. It is apparent that the Eton community, while it enjoys sport, is yet to become a preaching ground for an ideology of athleticism and militarism in the service of

[153]   Chandos, p. 321; Honey, *Tom Brown's Universe*, pp. 216-218.

empire.

A study of the *Chronicle* from 1928 reveals that, once again, sport maintains its dominant position, usually occupying between a half and three quarters of each issue. The non-sporting content contains much greater variety, revealing a broader range of intellectual and cultural activities available for the boys. There is also much more frequent mention of the role of masters in running activities. Again, similar to the first issues, there is no mention of empire. It can therefore be discerned that, by this stage, Eton had an unabashedly professionalized approach to the care of the boys and the running of all aspects of their lives at Eton. While games were as popular as ever, the school had nurtured a greater quantity and variety of non-sporting activities. While religion and domesticity are seldom referred to, there is also very little to reflect the values of muscular masculinity in the service of empire that was evident towards the end of the nineteenth century.

4.6 Conclusion

It has been shown that Eton reflects broader trends at work in Victorian England: 'the imperatives of empire' celebrating a 'militaristic and robust hypermasculinity'; reactions against effeminacy through the 'flight from domesticity' and the development of organized sports; the rise of the middle classes and the concomitant professionalization of various fields, including education; the upper classes becoming more actively involved in their children's upbringing.[154]

The values of athleticism and militarism formed a potent ideology within the Eton community. The content of the *Chronicle* frequently reflects this ideology and often explicitly champions it. While it belittles domesticity and ignores religion,

---

[154]   John Tosh, *A man's place: Masculinity and the middle-class home in Victorian England* (New Haven and London: Yale University Press, 1999); Francis, Martin, 'The domestication of the male? Recent research on nineteenth-and twentieth-century British masculinity', *The Historical Journal* 45.3 (2002): 637-652; Martin Daunton, *Wealth and Welfare: An Economic and Social History of Britain 1851-1951* (Oxford: Oxford University Press, 2007); John Gillis, *A World of Their Own Making: Myth, Ritual, and the Quest for Family Values* (Oxford: Oxford University Press, 1997).

the *Chronicle* sings the praises of bonds formed on the sports field and which would endure on the battlefield. This can be understood within the context of a ruling class that wanted able young men to venture away from home and family and commit to the service of the empire.[155] This serves as a further explanation of why increasing numbers of families aspired to send their sons to Eton.[156] Victorian Eton was a school which offered rigorous instruction in the classics and an increasing number of modern subjects, but, as this study has demonstrated, it was also a community in which boys had access to something not available at home: the opportunity to imbibe the masculine virtues and patriotic values of the ruling class, and learn to venture out and bring glory to their house, their school their empire and, in turn, to their families.

---

[155] Honey, *Tom Brown's Universe*, p. 115.

[156] See Appendix, Table 1.

5. Conclusions

This study has demonstrated that Eton changed considerably over the course of the Victorian period, both in terms of surface developments and in terms of the culture of the school. These changes were due to a range of factors sweeping through Victorian society, particularly the rise of the middle classes. The aristocratic 'liberties' prevalent at the start of the Victorian period were gradually overtaken by the 'intrusive and burdensome régime' which the middle classes were devising for their children.[157] Boys' leisure activities, a form of upper class conspicuous consumption, were co-opted by the school authorities as part of a broader effort to create a better supervised, more efficient system which

---

[157]   Tosh, 'Domesticity and Manliness in the Victorian Middle Class', p. 60.

would provide value for money in an England more and more dominated by middle class values.

At the beginning of the Victorian period, the 'liberties' were sacred, religion was central, and the culture of the school was best represented by the image of the young leisured aristocrat; by the end of the Victorian period, the leisured aristocrat was forced into dialogue with the striving bourgeois about the best way forward in an increasingly middle-class England presiding over a vast empire – a dialogue which resulted in the liberties and religion being supplanted by a 'secular trinity' of athleticism, militarism and imperialism.[158] While Eton had long provided an apprenticeship in external and internal masculine hegemony that would prepare its boys to exercise class and gender privilege, the increasingly professionalised and male-dominated (if not male-only) environment was rationalised through a rhetoric of nurturing 'Englishmen after the country's heart' (Warre). [159] At the start of the Victorian period, pupil

---

[158]   Mangan, *Athleticism*, p. 203.

[159]   Mack, vol. II, p. 127.

numbers were precarious; by the end, they had almost doubled and many more wanted to send their children to Eton. This was not just because the rise of the middle classes meant more people could aspire to a prestigious education for their sons. It was also because the provider of this education had made great changes in response to these families' expectations for their boys' education.

Appendix A: A Map of Modern Eton

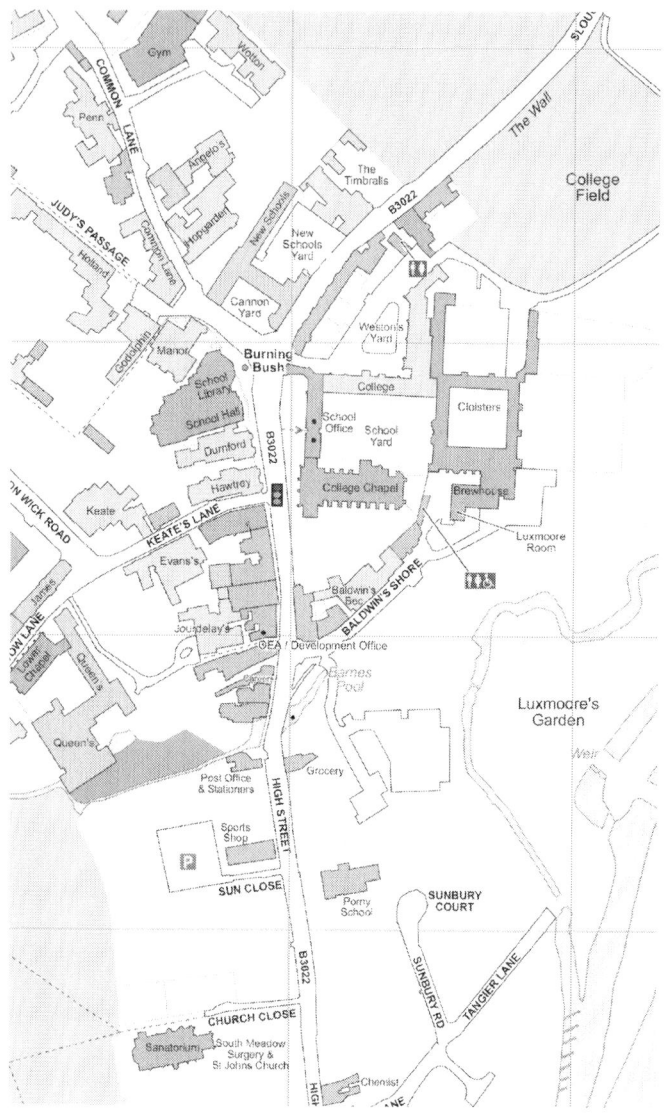

Appendix B: Pupil Population at Eton 1820-1910

1820: 528 boys

1830: 519 boys

1840: 593 boys

1850: 625 boys

1860: 820 boys

1870: 883 boys

1880: 895 boys

1890: 987 boys

1900: 1027 boys

1910: 1020 boys

Appendix C: Provosts and Head Masters 1750-1950

Provosts of Eton College 1750-1950

1746–1765   Stephen Sleech

1765–1781   Edward Barnard

1781–1791   William Hayward Roberts

1791–1809   Jonathan Davies

1809–1840   Joseph Goodall

1840–1853   Francis Hodgson

1853–1862   Edward Craven Hawtrey

1862–1884   Charles Old Goodford

1884–1909   James John Hornby

1909–1918   Edmond Warre

1918–1936   Montague Rhodes James

1936–1944   Lord Hugh Cecil

1945–1949   Sir Henry Marten

1949–1965   Sir Claude Aurelius Elliott

Head Masters of Eton College 1750-1950

1745–1754   John Sumner

1754–1765   Edward Barnard

1765–1773   John Foster

1773–1792   Jonathan Davies

1792–1802   George Heath

1802–1809   Joseph Goodall

1809–1834   John Keate

1834–1853   Edward Craven Hawtrey

1853–1862   Charles Old Goodford

1862–1868   Edward Balston

1868–1884   James John Hornby

1884–1905   Edmond Warre

1905–1916   Edward Lyttelton

1916–1933   Cyril Alington

1933–1949   Claude Aurelius Elliott

1949–1964   Robert Birley

Appendix D: Masters 1840-50

LIST OF

Provosts, Fellows, Masters, Assistant Masters, &c.

FROM 1840 TO 1850.

PROVOST.

Rev. Francis Hodgson, B.D., 1840[1]-32[1].

VICE-PROVOST.

Rev. John Septimus Grover, M.A. . . . . 1858-50[1]

FELLOWS.

Rev. George Bethell, M.A. . . 1818-50[2]	Rev. George Bowney Green, M.A. . 1835-60[1]	
Rev. John Francis Plumptree, M.A. . 1822-64[1]	Rev. George John Dupuis, M.A. . 1838-68[2]	
Rev. Thomas Carter, M.A. . . 1829-50[2]	Rev. John Wilder, M.A. . . . 1840[2]-84[1]	

STEWARDS OF THE COURTS.

John Goodheed Harris . . 1838-50[2] | Thomas Batchelor . . . 1850[2]-64[1]

HEAD MASTER.

Rev. Edward Craven Hawtrey, D.D. . . . 1834-32[2]

LOWER MASTERS.

Rev. Richard Okes, D.D. . 1839[2]-50[1] | Rev. Edward Coleridge, M.A. 1850[2]-50[2]

ASSISTANT MASTERS.

With Initials by which referred to in Lists.

Rev. Richard Okes, D.D. . 1821-88[2]	R.O.	Rev. Charles Luxmoore,	
Rev. John Wilder . . 1824-40	J.W.	M.A. . . . . 1823-83[1]	C.L.
Rev. Edward Coleridge,		Rev. William Gifford	
M.A. . . . . 1825-50[2]	E.C.	Cookesley, M.A. . . 1830-54[2]	W.G.C.

vi   LIST OF PROVOSTS, FELLOWS, MASTERS, ASSISTANT MASTERS, &c.

Rev. Edward Hayes Pickering, M.A.	1830-52¹	E.H.P.		Henry Mildred Birch, M.A.	1844⁵-43⁴	H.M.B.
Charles Wilder	1831-38	C.W.		Rev. William Colenso Davis, B.A., *Math.*	1845¹-46⁹	W.C.D.
Rev. Harry Dupuis, B.D.	1835-52²	H.D.		William Johnson (aft. Cory), M.A.	1845²-72⁵	W.J.
Rev. Charles Old Goodford, M.A.	1835-52³	C.O.G.		Rev. Robert Arrowsmith, B.A., *Math.*	1846⁹-40⁵	R.A.
Rev. William Laurence Eliot, M.A.	1836-62¹	W.L.E.		Rev. James Leigh Joynes, M.A.	1849⁶-77⁸	J.L.J.
Rev. Stephen Thomas Hawtrey, M.A., *Math.*	1836-78⁹	S.T.H.		Francis John Ottley, M.A., *Math.*	1849⁶-68¹	F.J.O.
Rev. Charles John Abraham, M.A.	1839-43⁵	C.J.A.		Rev. Wharton Booth Marriott, B.C.L.	1850⁴-60⁹	W.B.M.
Rev. William Adolphus Carter, M.A.	1839-57¹	W.A.C.		Rev. Charles Wolley (aft. Wolley-Dod), M.A.	1850⁴-79⁸	C.Wo.
Rev. Francis Edward Durnford, M.A.	1839-64¹	F.E.D.		Charles Chepmell, B.A., *Math.*	1850⁹-50⁷	C.C.
Rev. Edward Balston, M.A.	1840⁴-60⁵	E.B.		Rev. Edward Hale, M.A., F.G.S., *Math.*	1850⁹-94⁵	E.H.
Rev. John Eyre Yonge, M.A.	1840⁹-78⁴	J.E.Y.		Rev. Russell Day, M.A.	1851¹-74⁴	R.D.
Rev. John William Hawtrey, M.A.	1842-69⁵	J.W.H.		Rev. Augustus Frederick Birch, M.A.	1852⁴-64³	A.F.B.
Rev. Charles Ross de Havilland, M.A., *Math.*	1843⁵-44⁸	C.R.deH.		Rev. William Wayte, M.A.	1853⁵-73²	W.W.
Rev. George Frewer, M.A., *Math.*	1844¹-78⁹	G.F.				

EXTRA MASTERS.

Mr. Hexter	*Writing, Arith., and Maths.*	1823⁵-42⁹		Rev. Dr. Di Menna	*Italian*	1842⁸-42⁹
W. Evans	*Drawing*	1823⁵-43¹		Signor Girolamo Fochioni	*Italian*	1843⁵-48¹
H. Angelo	*Fencing*	1823⁵-64²		H. Tarver	*Assist. French Master*	1843⁵-51¹
Mr. Venua	*Dancing*	1824⁵-64³		Signor Sinibaldi	*Italian*	1848⁸-52³
Mr. Tarver	*French*	1830⁵-61¹		Samuel Evans	*Assist. Drawing Master*	1849⁹-53⁹
Mr. Schloerstedt	*German and Hebrew*	1830⁹-64¹				

Miss A.	= Miss Angelo		Mrs. Hol.	= Mrs. Holt		T.H.S.	= T. H. Stevens
Miss B.	= Miss Bourblock		R.F.H.	= R. F. Holt		Miss A. T. = Miss Ann Tyrrell
Mrs. de R. = Mrs. de Rosen		Mrs. Hor.	= Mrs. Hereford		Mrs. Vall. = Mrs. Vallancey
Mrs. D.	= Mrs. Dodd		Miss M.	= Miss Middleton		Mrs. Vav. = Mrs. Vavasour
Mrs. Dr.	= Mrs. Drury		Mrs. P.	= Mrs. Parker		Mrs. Vo. = Mrs. Voysey
Miss Edg. = Miss Edgar		Mrs. Ri.	= Mrs. Rishton		F.V.	= Rev. F. Vidal
Miss Edw. = Miss Edwards		Mrs. Ro.	= Mrs. Roberts (née Slingsby)		Miss W.	= Miss Ward
W.E.	= W. Evans					Mrs. Y.	= Mrs. Yonge
Miss G.	= Miss Gulliver		Misses S. = Misses Slingsby		

K.S. = King's Scholar.

Appendix E: Masters 1890-1900

LIST OF

𝕻rovosts, 𝕱ellows, 𝕸asters, 𝕬ssistant 𝕸asters, &c.

FROM 1890—1900.

PROVOST.

Rev. James John Hornby, D.D., D.C.L., C.V.O. . . . 1884¹-1909²

VICE-PROVOSTS.

Rev. John Wilder, M.A. 1885¹-92²
Francis Warre Cornish, M.A. 1893²

FELLOWS.

Ven. Archdeacon Edward Balston, D.D. 1860²-61³
  „ „ „ „ „ 1908¹-91¹
Rev. William Adolphus Carter, M.A. 1854²-1901²
Rt. Hon. Spencer Horatio Walpole,
  LL.D., Q.C., M.P. . . . 1871¹-96²
The Earl of Morley, B.A. . . . 1871¹-1905²
Sir William Reynell Anson, Bart.,
  M.P., D.C.L. (Warden of All
  Souls' College, Oxford) . . 1884²
Rev. Norman Macleod Ferrers, D.D.,
  F.R.S. (Master of Gonville and
  Caius College, Cambridge) . 1886¹-96¹
Rt. Rev. Randall Thomas Davidson,
  D.D. (Bishop of Winchester) . 1887¹-96²
Hon. George Charles Brodrick, M.A.
  (Warden of Merton College,
  Oxford) 1888¹-1903²
Sir Henry Enfield Roscoe, Kt.,
  D.C.L., F.R.S., LL.D. . . 1889²

Rev. Augustus Austen Leigh, M.A.
  (Provost of King's College, Cam-
  bridge) 1889²-1905¹
Rt. Hon. Sir Charles Synge Christo-
  pher Bowen, D.C.L. (Lord
  Justice of Appeal) . . . 1889¹-94¹
The Viscount Cobham, M.A. . . 1891¹
Rt. Hon. Lord Herschell, G.C.B.,
  D.C.L., LL.D. (Lord High
  Chancellor) 1894²-99¹
Charles Smith, M.A. (Master of
  Sidney Sussex College, Cam-
  bridge) 1896²
Rt. Hon. the Earl of Halsbury,
  F.R.S., M.A. (Lord High
  Chancellor) 1899²
Hon. W. F. D. Smith, M.P. . . 1902

CONDUCTS.

Rev. Frederick Meredith Hargreaves, M.A. . . . 1894[2]-1909[3]
Rev. George Sevier Davies, M.A. . . . . . 1887[1]-1912[1]
Rev. Harold Sydney Vinning, M.A. . . . . . 1909[6]-1915[3]

PRECENTOR AND MUSICAL INSTRUCTOR.

Charles Harford Lloyd, M.A., Mus.Doc. . . . . 1892[5]-1914[1]

STEWARD OF THE COURTS.

Sir Frederick Albert Bosanquet, M.A., K.C. . . . . . 1899[5]

DEPUTY-STEWARD OF THE COURTS.

H. A. Carter . . . . 1906[1]

BURSAR.

Henry Calthrop Hollway-Calthrop . . . . . . 1906[5]-1918[3]

JUNIOR BURSAR AND SCHOOL FUND ACCOUNTANT.

Patrick Arthur Macindoe, C.A. . . . . . . 1906[1]-1918[3]

AUDITORS.

Thomas Frederick Kirby . . . . 1891[3]-1901[1]
Sir William Plender, G.B.E., F.C.A. (of the firm of Deloitte, Plender, Griffiths & Co.) . . . . 1901[1]

CLERK TO THE PROVOST AND FELLOWS.

Harry Berwick Dyke . . . . 1900[6]

HEAD MASTERS.

Rev. Edmond Warre, D.D., D.C.L., C.B., C.V.O. . . . . 1884[5]-1905[1]
Rev. the Hon. Edward Lyttelton, D.D. . . . . . 1905[3]-1916[1]

LOWER MASTERS.

Edward Compton Austen Leigh, M.A. . . . . 1887[3]-1905[2] E.C.A.L.
Francis Hay Rawlins, M.A. . . . . . . 1905[5]-1916[3] F.H.R.

ASSISTANT MASTERS.

With Initials by which referred to in Lists.

Edward Peake Rouse, M.A., *Math.* . . . 1861[5]-1901[3] E.P.R.	Rev. Raymond Cone Radcliffe, M.A., *Math. and Classics* . . . 1872[5]-1907[1] R.C.R.	
Arthur Campbell Ainger, M.A., M.V.O. . . . 1864[9]-1901[3] A.C.A.	Henry Broadbent, M.A., *Class.* . . . 1876[1]-1919[1] H.B.	
Henry Elford Luxmoore, M.A. . . . . 1864[5]-1908[1] H.E.L.	Edward Littleton Vaughan, M.A. . . . 1876[3]-1913[3] E.L.V.	
Richard Arthur Henry Mitchell, M.A. . . 1866[3]-1901[3] R.A.H.M.	Rev. Stuart Alexander Donaldson, M.A. . 1878[1]-1904[2] S.A.D.	
Thomas John Proctor Carter, M.A., *Math.* . 1858[5]-99[3] J.P.C.	Philip Williams, M.A., *Math. and German* . 1878[3]-1911[3] P.W.	
Francis Hay Rawlins, M.A. (Lower Master) . 1875[3]-1905[2] F.H.R.	Charles Lowry, M.A. . 1883[5]-1900[5] C.L.	
	Edward Impey, M.A. . 1884[1]-1913[3] E.I.	

97

LIST OF PROVOSTS, FELLOWS, MASTERS, ASSISTANT MASTERS, &c.   vii

Charles Howard Allcock, M.A., *Math.* . . 1884³–1910¹ C.H.A.

Arthur Christopher Benson, C.V.O., M.A., F.R.Hist.S. . . 1885¹–1903⁶ A.C.B.

Annesley Ashworth Somerville, M.A., *Math. and French* . . 1885¹ A.A.S.

John Hugh Montagu Hare, M.A., *Class.* . 1885¹ J.H.M.H.

Richard Adolf Ploetz, M.A., *German* . . 1885²–1901³ R.A.P.

Thomas Cunningham Porter, M.A., D.Sc., F.C.S., F.R.A.S., F.Ph.S.Lond., M.R.I., F.R.P.S., *Science* 1885² T.C.P.

Remington Walter White-Thomson, M.A. . . 1885³–1905⁶ R.W.W.-T.

Herbert Francis William Tatham, M.A. . . 1886¹–1909⁶ H.F.W.T.

Hugh Vibart Macnaghten, M.A., *Class.* . . 1886²–1920⁶ H.M.

Hubert Brinton, M.A., *Class.* . . . 1887¹ H.Br.

Arthur Conolly Gage Heygate, M.A., *Class.* . 1887³–1918⁶ A.C.G.H.

Rev. Henry Thomas Bowlby, M.A. . . . 1887³–1909⁶ H.T.B.

Rev. Lionel George Bridges Justice Ford, M.A. . . . 1888¹–1901³ L.F.

Robert Fenrice Lee Booker, M.A., F.S.A., *Class.* . . . 1888¹–1920⁶ R.P.L.B.

John Maximilian Dyer, M.A., *Math.* . . 1889⁶–1911³ J.M.D.

Richard Stephen Kindersley, M.A., *Class.* . 1889⁶–1920¹ R.S.K.

Reginald Saumarez de Havilland, M.A., V.D., *Math. and History* . 1889⁶–1920⁶ R.S.deH.

Arthur Murray Goodhart, M.A., Mus. Bac., *Class.* 1889¹ A.M.G.

Lionel Stanley Rice Byron, M.A., *French and German* . 1889² L.S.R.B.

Edward Wellington Stone, M.A., *Class.* . . 1890² E.W.S.

Philip Vere Broke, M.A., *Math.* . . . 1891³–1917³ P.V.B.

Cyril Mowbray Wells, B.A., *Class.* . 1893² C.M.W.

William Sidney Vernon Evans, *Drawing* . . 1893³–1922⁶

Ernest Lee Churchill, B.A., *Class.* . . . 1893⁶ E.L.C.

Gilbert Harrison John Hurst, M.A., F.C.P.S., F.Ph.S.Lond., *Math.* . 1894⁶–1903⁶ G.H.J.H.

William Douglas Eggar, M.A., *Science* . 1895¹–1920⁶ W.D.E.

Allen Beville Ramsay, M.A., *Class.* . . 1895²–1916⁶ A.B.R.

Jean Philippe Auguste Cuvelier, *French* . 1896¹–1915² J.P.A.C.

Matthew Davenport Hill, M.A., *Science* . . 1896¹ M.D.H.

Clarence Henry Kennett Marten, M.A., *History* . 1896² C.H.K.M.

Hugh de Havilland, M.A., *Science* . . . 1897³–1919⁶ H.deH.

Samuel Gurney Lubbock, M.A., *Class.* . 1897¹ S.G.L.

Alfred Edward Conybeare, M.A., *Math.* . 1897² A.E.C.

Vivian Le Neve Foster, M.A., *Math.* . . 1898¹–1920⁶ V.LeN.F.

Algernon Cockburn Rayner-Wood, M.A., *Class., French and German* . 1898¹ A.C.R.-W.

Frederick Eden Robeson, M.A., *Class., French and German* . . . 1899⁶ F.E.R.

Rev. Cyril Argentine Alington, M.A. . . 1899²–1908³ C.A.A.

Thomas Frank Cattley, M.A., *Class.* . . 1899² T.F.C.

Paul Snoones, B.A., *Math.* 1899⁶–1914² P.S.

Reymond Hervey de Montmorency, M.A., *French, German and Spanish* . . 1900⁶ R.H.deM.

Leonard Todd, M.A., *Math.* . . . 1900⁶ L.T.

Francis Wellesley Dobbs, M.A., *Math.* . . 1900⁶ F.W.D.

Aymer William Whitworth, M.A., *Class.* . 1901¹ A.W.W.

William Theodore Douglas Bolton, M.A., *Math.* 1901³–1919⁶ W.T.D.B.

Hugh Michael Bland, M.A., *French* . . 1901¹ H.M.B.

Rev. George Jameson Chitty, M.A., *Class.* . 1901¹ G.J.C.

John Foster Crace, M.A., *Class.* . . . 1901¹ J.F.C.

Charles Lancelot Stocks, B.A. . . . 1901³–1901³ C.L.S.

viii   LIST OF PROVOSTS, FELLOWS, MASTERS, ASSISTANT MASTERS, &c.

Rev. Charles Robert
Lorraine   McDowall,
M.A.   .   .   .   .1902²-1910²C.R.L.McD.
Archibald Magne Mc
Neile, M.A., Math.   .   1902¹   A.M.McN.
Geoffrey Winthrop Young,
M.A., German   .   1902²-1903² G.W.Y.
Edward Vere Slater, M.A.,
Class.   .   .   .   1903²   E.V.S.
Edmund Arnold Alfred
Spencer, M.A.   .   1903²-1903² E.A.A.S.
Philippe Cosme Henri de
Satgé, B. ès L., French   1903²   P.C.H.deS.
Rev. Francis Granville
Channon, M.A., Math.   1904¹   F.G.C.
Geoffrey Wycliffe Head-
lam, B.A., Class. and
History   .   .   .   1904²   G.W.H.
Cuthbert Harold Eakin-
son, M.A., Class.   .   1904²   C.H.E.
Brian Charles Harrison,
B.A., Class.   .   1904¹-1905² B.C.H.
Rev. Charles Oliver Bevan,
M.A., Class.   .   1905²   C.O.B.
Clement James Mellish
Adie, M.A., French and
German   .   .   1905²   C.J.M.A.
David Henry Loch, B.A.,
French and German   1905²-1906² D.H.L.
Ralph Butler, B.A., Class.   1906²-1906² R.B.
Charles Worrall Carring-
ton, B.A., Class.   .   1906¹-1907¹ C.W.C.
George Leonard Nelson
Hope, B.A., French
and German   .   1906²-1906² G.L.N.H.
Rev. Lionel Bethell
Trenchard Chaffey,
M.A., French and Ger-
man   .   .   .   1906²   L.B.T.C.
Rev. John Chaloner Chute,
M.A., Math.   .   1906²   J.C.C.
Noel Roy Dalacour
Tennant, B.A., French
and German   .   1906²-1906² N.R.D.T.
John Christie, M.A.,
Math. and Science   .   1906¹   J.C.
Robert Balmain Mowat,
B.A., History   .   1906²-1907¹ R.B.M.
Arthur Charles Sheep-
shanks, B.A., D.S.O.,
Class.   .   .   .   1907¹   A.C.S.
William Hope-Jones, B.A.,
Math.   .   .   .   1907²   W.H.-J.

Francis Robinson Glad-
stone Duckworth, M.A.,
Class.   .   .   1908²-1919² F.R.G.D.
Hon. George William
Lyttelton, B.A., Class.   1908²   G.W.L.
Richard Selby Durnford,
B.A., Class.   .   1909²-1912² R.S.D.
William Douglas Pennock
Hill, B.A., Class.   .   1909²-1912² W.D.P.H.
Eric Walter Powell, B.A.,
O.B.E., French and Ger-
man   .   .   .   1910²   E.W.P.
Richard Alfred Young,
B.A., Math.   .   1910²   R.A.Y.
Richard Oliver Walpole
Pemberton, B.A., French
and German   .   1910²-1910² R.O.W.P.
William Donald Campbell
Laidlaw Pavene, B.A.,
French and German   .1911¹-1912² W.D.C.L.P.
Hugh Kenyon Marsden,
M.A., Math.   .   1912¹   H.K.M.
Robert Francis Mudie,
B.A., Math.   .   1912²-1913² R.F.M.
Charles Andrew Glad-
stone, B.A., French,
German and Russian   1912²   C.A.G.
Edward Foss Prior, M.A.,
Class.   .   .   1912²-1916² E.F.P.
Reginald   Montague
Wright, M.A., Math.   1913²   R.M.W.
Walter George Fletcher,
M.A., Class.   .   1913²-1915² W.G.F.
Cyril Hackett Wilkinson,
B.A., French and
History   .   .   1913²-1915² C.H.W.

M.G. Huc, M.V.O., French   1882²-1903²
Signor V. de Asarta, Italian   1881²-1909²
Samuel Thomas George
Evans, A.R.W.S., Draw-
ing   .   .   .   1854²-1903²
Gustav Morush, A. of Co-
logne, Assistant Musical
Instructor   .   .   1903²-1906²
Lieut. Bernard Trotter
Coote, R.N. (Ret.), Gym-
nastics   .   .   1910²-1915²
Reginald Edward Roper,
M.A., Gymnastics   .   1910²-1915²

Miss E. = Miss Evans
K.S.   = King's Scholar

99

Appendix F: Data from the *Eton College Chronicle*

Table 1: The number of articles reflecting values that might be emphasized in a boarding school community.[160]

	Athleticism	Militarism	Domesticity	Intellectualism /Aestheticism	Religion
390 3 Oct 1884	13	0	0	9	1
391 16 Oct 1884	14	1+	1	7	2
392 30 Oct 1884	7	1	1	6	(1)
810 22 Sep 1898	18	3	1	4	0
811 29 Sep 1898	10	3	0	3	1
812 6 Oct 1898	11	1+	1	6	0

The figures in this table are for each piece (report, letter or other article), regardless of length, that corresponds to the theme in the column heading.

---

[160]   Data from the case study in Chapter 4.

Some pieces corresponded to more than one, and so may be counted twice. This method revealed the prominence of each theme. A decision had to be made as to whether to measure the number of pieces per theme or the amount of column space. It was decided to measure the former, as each report reflects one event taking place in the life of the school. Judging prominence according to column space would have, for example, given a lengthy report on an evening of debating involving around 20 boys more prominence than a short report on an afternoon of cricket involving the same number of boys.

'+' = particularly lengthy and detailed reports on ECRV field days that will have involved a very large number of boys.

'(1)' = a letter complaining that people standing up at the wrong time in Chapel means that the writer cannot hear the anthem properly – more aesthetic than religious in its emphasis.

Table 2: The number of articles which mention older boys taking charge of school activities (in the spirit of the traditional 'liberties'), as compared to the number of articles which showcase the involvement of masters.[161]

	Liberties	Masters
390 3 Oct 1884	2	5
391 16 Oct 1884	3	2
392 30 Oct 1884	3	2
810 22 Sep 1898	2	1
811 29 Sep 1898	1	4
812 6 Oct 1898	3	2

---

[161] Data from the case study in Chapter 4.

Appendix G: Historiographical note on debates, sources and methods

Introduction

Integral to an understanding of the Victorian family is a consideration of the rise of the public schools. These were communities where an increasing number of English families felt their boys ought to spend much of their adolescence.[162] Historians of education tell of many changes over the Victorian period: the development of the public school system; the emergence of the cult of games; the broadening of the curriculum; the establishment of rifle volunteers; the demise of boy rebellions; greater supervision by masters; and attempts to encourage arts and music.[163]

---

[162]   Vivian Ogilvie, *The English Public School* (London: Batsford, 1957), pp. 139-179; John Honey, *Tom Brown's Universe: The Development of the Victorian Public School* (London: Millington, 1977), pp. 238-247.

[163]   Edward C. Mack, *Public Schools and British Opinion Volume I (1780-1860)* (London: Methuen, 1938) and *Public Schools and British Opinion Volume II (Since 1860)* (New York: Columbia University Press, 1941); T. W. Bamford, *Rise of the Public Schools* (London: Nelson, 1967); Jonathan Gathorne-Hardy, *The Public School Phenomenon* (London : Hodder and Stoughton, 1977); Honey,

Yet studies approaching the topic from the perspective of the history of the family argue that very little changed.[164] This is partly a matter of the sources and perspectives used: historians of education have their attention drawn to key changes, due to their use of documentary and material evidence produced within schools, as well as debates on educational reform; the historians of the family cited make use of letters and journals, finding broader consistency in subject matter over a long period of time.

This study aims to bridge this divide. French and Rothery suggest a way forward through their use of Braudel's three levels of historical occurrence: at the deepest level, that of 'structure', geographical and cultural processes take place over the course of centuries and millennia; the uppermost level is that of '*événements*', events and actions involving particular people in particular places, within a timeframe of days

---

Tom Brown's Universe; John Chandos, *Boys Together: English Public Schools 1800-1864* (London: Hutchinson, 1984).

[164]   Anthony Fletcher, *Growing up in England: The Experience of Childhood, 1600-1914* (New Haven and London: Yale University Press, 2008), p. 197; Henry French and Mark Rothery, *Man's Estate: Landed Gentry Masculinities 1660-1900* (Oxford: Oxford University Press, 2012), p. 78.

and years; in between, Braudel identified the level of *'conjoncture'*, which can be understood as a point of engagement between deeply rooted structures and surface *événements*, and which can be analysed through ideas and values over the course of decades and centuries.[165] French and Rothery draw on Braudel's three levels for their study of English gentry families from 1660 to 1900, devoting particular attention to the conjunctural level. They see it as the point at which deeply established patriarchal principles interacted with everyday lived realities, resulting in discourses (as expressed, for French and Rothery's study, in family letters) through which can be traced the formation of various, often competing, conceptions of masculinity.[166] It therefore becomes clear that historians of education focus on surface events with some reference to the conjunctural level, while historians of the family focus on the conjunctural level with reference to underlying structures. This explains why one perspective suggests much change, while the other suggests broader

---

[165]   Pierre Daix, *Braudel* (Paris: Flammarion, 1995), p. 170.

[166]   French and Rothery, pp. 11-12.

continuity. If one combines both types of analysis, a fuller picture emerges.

Some studies of education combine the school and family history approaches, researching changes on the surface and linking this with analysis of ideas at the conjunctural level, even if they don't cite Braudel's model. Newsome undertakes an exploration of Victorian values by analysing their underlying ideas as articulated within the world of public schools, noting a shift in ideals over the period from godliness and good learning to Muscular Christianity and its cult of manliness, games and empire.[167] Honey sees the notion of manliness as key to the 'transfer of function' from family to school over the Victorian period.[168] By the second half of the nineteenth century, it became a consensus that the characteristics and qualifications of a successful gentleman could only be acquired through a public school education

[167]   David Newsome, *Godliness and Good Learning: Four Studies on a Victorian Ideal* (London: John Murray, 1961), p. 198.

[168]   Honey, 'Tom Brown's Universe: The Nature and Limits of the Victorian Public Schools Community' in *The Victorian Public School: Studies in the Development of an Educational Institution* ed. by Brian Simon and Ian Bradley (Dublin: Gill and Macmillan, 1975), pp. 19-33 (p. 21).

and so this 'became the common experience of the sons of the English upper classes'.[169] Honey notes the 'completeness of the transfer to an alternative community – a distinctive social milieu capable of generating its own set of values [...]'.[170]

This identification of broader trends by Newsome and Honey points to another divide in studies of Victorian public schools: that between the national and the local. With wealthy families keeping useful records for historians of Victorian England, there is an abundance of evidence, yet it is mostly used for general rather than localised studies. Histories of education or of the family in Victorian England refer to episodes from Eton when they fit in with the overall narrative.[171] Studies cite letters home from Eton or reminiscences by former Etonians, weaving them into a general account.[172] Prominent are anecdotes of the birch-wielding Keate (head master

---

[169]   Honey, *Tom Brown's Universe* (1977), p. 146.

[170]   Ibid. , p. 147.

[171]   Mack, vols I and II; Gathorne-Hardy; Honey, *Tom Brown's Universe.*

[172]   Fletcher, *Growing up in England,* p. 182; French and Rothery, p. 55.

1809-1834), whose brutal ways provided memories in which, according to Fletcher, the Victorian governing class 'found the very essence of its being'.[173] Meanwhile, of the two principal histories of Eton, one was composed during the late-nineteenth century and is stronger on earlier periods, while the other's section on the Victorian age is dominated by public debate for reform, revolving around the Clarendon Commission of 1861-4.[174] This present work seeks to answer the need for a focused local case study of Victorian Eton, which analyses realities on the ground while linking them to national trends.

Mangan discusses the implications for research methods of the abundance of evidence for public schools. Following up on Honey's research, Mangan focuses on the 'rise of the games cult', which became central to the notion of the public school as a community.[175] He does, however, raise a

---

[173]   Fletcher, *Growing up in England*, p. 317; Ogilvie, ch. IX; Chandos, ch. 10.

[174]   Tim Card, *Eton Renewed: A History from 1860 to the present day* (London: John Murray, 1994), ch. 2.

[175]   Honey, *Tom Brown's Universe* (1977), p. 104.

methodological concern: Honey's 'sampling universe' of evidence is the whole public school system, whereas a more systematic approach is required, separating rhetoric from empirical realities.[176] He therefore engages in an intensive-comparative analysis of sources from the Victorian and Edwardian periods for a representative sample of six public schools (not including Eton). He finds that the imposition of an extensive programme of compulsory games was a means of managing the historic problem of indiscipline and the modern problem of increasing pupil numbers, owing to the growth in families desiring a public school education for their sons.[177] He distinguishes between these facts on the ground and the rationalisations given, going on to devote a whole chapter to analysing the rhetoric surrounding games.[178] This is an example to follow for Eton, with separate analyses of developments on the ground (Braudel's upper level) and surrounding rhetoric (emanating from Braudel's middle level).

---

[176]   James Mangan, *Athleticism in the Victorian and Edwardian Public School* (London: Routledge, 2012), p. 3.

[177]   Ibid. , p. 28.

[178]   Ibid, p. 24 and pp. 179-206.

There are some further reasons for a case study of Victorian Eton which are related to the study of masculinity. Tosh describes the rise of the public schools as 'one of the most significant shifts in the culture of manliness in the nineteenth century.'[179] Eton is taken as being emblematic of this Victorian phenomenon, and yet there is no local case study. Furthermore, in his review essay, Francis made a call for further research that is particularly relevant to this study.[180] He noted a need for work on middle-class masculinity over the last two hundred years (notably by Tosh) to be supplemented with studies of aristocratic and working-class forms of manly behaviour. For example, investigating the creative tension between aristocratic and bourgeois genres of masculinity would reveal the processes at work in the broadening of the notion of the 'gentleman' in the twentieth century. In public schools, the interplay between aristocratic and bourgeois stereotypes is

---

[179]   John Tosh, *A Man's Place: Masculinity and the Middle-Class Home in Victorian England* (New Haven and London: Yale University Press, 2007), p. 117.

[180]   Martin Francis, 'The domestication of the male? Recent research on nineteenth-and twentieth-century British masculinity', *The Historical Journal*, Vol. 45, No. 3 (2002), 637-652 (p. 652).

much in evidence in the nineteenth century, as sons of established families sought to negotiate their entry into a world which required them to pass exams and apply for jobs, while sons of the newly rich sought to find their place in the social elite. From Eton more than any other school, with its high concentration of boys from aristocratic families, it is be possible to provide a perspective which supplements work that has focused on the middle classes.

Aim and Method

This study aims to conduct a locally-based analysis of Victorian Eton, assessing the extent to which it was changed by broader social trends. Applying French and Rothery's adaptation of Braudel's three-level model of historical occurrence, it seeks to analyse the surface level of events separately from an analysis of values competing at the conjunctural level. Bringing these two analyses together results in a more rounded and nuanced picture. Furthermore, using Mangan's source-intensive yet contextualised approach, it undertakes a focused local analysis that is linked to broader themes. This brings out the extent to which Eton was part of the changes sweeping through Victorian society, while also making clear the role of local factors.

First, it looks at the upper level of *événements*, analysing surface changes at Eton over the Victorian period. This is divided into topographical developments (Chapter 2) and the roles played by different members of the community (Chapter 3). Understanding how the space changed and then how the people in that space changed yields a detailed understanding of developments at Eton over the Victorian period. The method is comparative, focusing on differences between the start of the period (under the headmastership of Edward Craven Hawtrey, 1834-1853) and the end of the period (under the headmastership of Edmond Warre, 1884-1905). In order to understand whether these changes are due more to broader or local factors, the effect of the following broader trends is assessed throughout the analysis: the revolution in transport and communications;[181] the family becoming an affectional base even as it became physically dispersed;[182] the ideal of domesticity;[183] the closer supervision of children;[184] secularisation;[185] professionalisation of various roles, including schoolteaching;[186] and the cults of athleticism and empire.[187]

The aim of Chapters 2 and 3 is to fill certain gaps in historians' treatments of Eton and similar schools. There is a tendency in studies of the Victorian family to treat public schools like Eton as constants.[188] Whether the study is arguing for

---

[181]   Bamford , p. 60.

[182]   John R. Gillis, *A World of Their Own Making: Myth, Ritual, and the Quest for Family Values* (Harvard: Harvard University Press, 1997), p. 71.

[183]   Tosh, *A Man's Place*, pp. 13-14.

[184]   Ibid., p. 60.

[185]   Hugh McLeod, *Secularisation in Western Europe, 1848–1914*. (Basingstoke: Macmillan, 2000).

[186]   Harold Perkin, *The Rise of the Professional Society: England since 1880* (London: Routledge, 2003), p. xii.

[187]   Mangan, *Athleticism*.

[188]   David Roberts, 'The *Paterfamilias* of the Victorian Governing Class' in *The Victorian Family*, ed. by Anthony S. Wohl (Beckenham: Croom Helm, 1978); J. A. Banks, *Victorian Values: Secularism and the Size of Families* (London: Routledge & Kegan Paul, 1981); Fletcher, *Growing up in England*; French and Rothery.

continuity or change within the area it addresses, there is an underlying assumption, when referring to boys' education, that 'nothing changed in the culture of the public schools between the 1000s and 1914'.[189] This is in part due to the sources used, as letters and journals foreground personal concerns and do not say as much about changing conditions as, for example, administrative documents and architectural developments. As for studies of Victorian public schools from the perspective of educational history, these do note changes, but there is a dominant narrative which focuses on the cult of games, with Eton and other public schools turning into a factory for privileged philistines who could run an empire.[190] Another narrative, often found in histories of Eton itself, is built around Victorian reforms in governance and curriculum, giving prominence to the Clarendon Commission.[191] The case studies in Chapters 2 and 3 demonstrate that these approaches, while serviceable

---

[189]   Fletcher, *Growing up in England*, p. 197.

[190]   Mack, vols I and II; also Mangan, *Athleticism*, Chandos; and Newsome.

[191]   Maxwell Lyte, *A History of Eton College 1440-1910* (London: Macmillan, 1911); Card, *Eton Renewed*.

in many ways, ignore other aspects of Eton over the
Victorian period: the role of the rise of middle class
culture, especially through domesticity and
professionalisation; the role of other broader trends,
such as changes in technology and the growing
secularisation of the country; and the way in which
these broader trends interacted with local factors
within Eton. It is argued that a broad range of
changes took place at Eton over the course of the
Victorian period, principally because it was fully
subject to the broader trends sweeping through the
country. Moreover, Braudel's three-level model is
useful here as these treatments of public schools can
tend to conflate the upper level of surface
occurrences and the middle, conjunctural level where
ideas and values are formed. Chapters 2 and 3 use
architectural and administrative sources to show that,
at least on the upper level, significant changes
occurred.

In Chapters 2 and 3, some changes in values
and culture are discussed. These more properly
belong to Braudel's middle, conjunctural level and

Chapter 4 focuses on this. On Braudel's middle level of *conjoncture*, the 'profound ordering principle' of patriarchal power at the deeper level interacts with cultural discourses to produce a set of values which boys needed to negotiate as part of the development of their gender identity.[192] Scholarship on family in general and masculinity in particular has mentioned a number of values as competing for influence during this period: athleticism; militarism (including empire); aestheticism and intellectualism (considered together); domesticity and religion.[193] Some of these values were dominant, but none were hegemonic, and each boy had to negotiate them in order to develop his gender identity. Newsome posits a cultural shift in public schools over the course of the Victorian period, from the dominance of godliness and good learning to the cult of athleticism, militarism and empire.[194] It

---

[192]   French and Rothery, p. 12.

[193]   Tosh, *A Man's Place*; Martin, 'The domestication of the male?'; Leonore Davidoff and Catherine Hall, *Family Fortunes* (Oxford: Routledge, 2002); Lesley A. Hall, *Sex, Gender and Social Change in Britain since 1880* (Basingstoke: Palgrave, 2013).

[194]   Newsome, p. 198.

becomes apparent that developments at Eton closely conform to this model.

Chapter 4 uses the *Eton College Chronicle* as a source for the nature of the community to which an increasing number of late-Victorian families aspired to send their sons.[195] (Mangan notes that school magazines are repositories of school values.[196]) It focuses on issues from Eton under Edmond Warre (Head Master 1884-1905), including a comparative analysis of issues from the start and towards the end of his tenure. This is a different approach to the previous two chapters, which compare Eton at the start and end of the Victorian period. As the *Chronicle* started in 1863, using that approach would have required comparing different types of source. This is a source-intensive analysis and consistency in material is required. Warre's tenure was chosen as, by 1884, the *Chronicle* had developed the format which it would continue to have until the mid-twentieth century. Moreover, it becomes apparent that, even within

---

[195]   See Appendix B. Also: Ogilvie, pp. 139-179; Honey, *Tom Brown's Universe*, ch. 4.

[196]   Mangan, *Athleticism*, pp. 243-250.

these two decades, considerable change in the culture of the school can be discerned. For the sake of broader context, earlier and later issues of the *Chronicle* are also analysed.

Chapter 4 demonstrates that Eton broadly fits Newsome's model of a shift from godliness to manliness. The context from earlier and later issues reveals that this trend peaked at the end of the Victorian period. Moreover, it is shown that Eton reflects national trends on Braudel's middle, conjunctural level of ideas and values formed over decades and centuries: 'the imperatives of empire' celebrating a 'militaristic and robust hypermasculinity'; reactions against effeminacy through the 'flight from domesticity' and the development of organized sports; the rise of the middle classes and the concomitant professionalization of various fields, including education; the upper classes becoming more actively involved in their children's upbringing.[197]

---

[197]   John Tosh, *A man's place: Masculinity and the middle-class home in Victorian England* (New Haven and London: Yale University Press, 1999); Francis, Martin, 'The domestication of the male? Recent research on nineteenth-and twentieth-century British masculinity', *The Historical Journal* 45.3 (2002): 637-652; Martin

The values of athleticism and militarism formed a potent ideology within the Eton community. The content of the *Chronicle* frequently reflects this ideology and often explicitly champions it. While it belittles domesticity and ignores religion, the *Chronicle* sings the praises of bonds formed on the sports field and which would endure on the battlefield. This can be understood within the context of a ruling class that wanted able young men to venture away from home and family and commit to the service of the empire.[198] This serves as a further explanation of why increasing numbers of families aspired to send their sons to Eton.[199] Victorian Eton was a school which offered rigorous instruction in the classics and an increasing number of modern subjects, but, as this study has demonstrated, it was also a community in which boys had access to something not available at home: the opportunity to imbibe the

---

Daunton, *Wealth and Welfare: An Economic and Social History of Britain 1851-1951* (Oxford: Oxford University Press, 2007); John Gillis, *A World of Their Own Making: Myth, Ritual, and the Quest for Family Values* (Oxford: Oxford University Press, 1997).

[198]   Honey, *Tom Brown's Universe*, p. 115.

[199]   See Appendix, Table 1.

masculine virtues and patriotic values of the ruling class, and learn to venture out and bring glory to their house, their school their empire and, in turn, to their families.

Arguments

This study argues that Eton changed significantly over the Victorian period. If one relied on family letters, journals and memoirs, then a good deal of continuity would be discerned. However, analysis of topographical changes and administrative documents within Eton, viewed in the context of broader social trends, demonstrates significant developments on the surface level; an analysis of the school magazine demonstrates changes in values on the conjunctural level, not just over the course of the Victorian period but even between the 1880s and the 1890s. Furthermore, this study will acknowledge that Newsome's model of godliness to manliness holds true for Eton, although sport was always high on the agenda, and there was rather less godliness to start off with, eventually giving way to a creed centered around a 'secular trinity'[200] of athleticism, militarism and empire.

Rather than understanding Eton as a fortress of tradition resisting modernity, it is more fitting to see it as being subject to the same broader forces that were at work throughout English society. Principal among these was the rise of the middle classes. Related to this were a number of other key trends, such as domesticity and professionalisation. In terms of demographics, Eton remained the most aristocratic of schools. However, middle class values had begun to permeate. Changes in the curriculum and more formalised examinations could be seen as supporting Tosh's thesis about the dominance of middle-class values, yet, in the case of Eton, there is a tension (often creative) with more established aristocratic values expressed through an emphasis on leisure and role models who exuded effortless superiority. Indeed, while the increased professionalisation of the school and greater supervision of the boys can be seen as reflections of middle class culture, the cult of

---

[200]   Ibid., p. 203.

games, militarism and empire can be seen as policies intended to serve the needs of the upper classes. Both tendencies marked major changes in the life and culture of the Eton community, even if they were not entirely in harmony.

Bibliography

Primary Sources (unpublished)

Eton College Archives

> COLL/P13 Edward Craven Hawtrey papers.
>
> COLL/P05 Edmond Warre papers.
>
> ED 383 Herbert family letters
>
> ED 354 Herbert family papers
>
> ED 351 Spicer family letters
>
> ED 67 04 Christie-Miller family letters
>
> Briscoe, John ,'555 years of Medical Care at Eton' (unpublished lecture, ECA, 1996)
>
> *Eton College Chronicle*

Primary Sources (published)

Ainger, Arthur Campbell, *Memories of Eton Sixty Ago* (London: John Murray, 1917).

Alington, C. A., *Things Ancient and Modern* (London: Longmans, Green and Co. , 1936).

An Old Colleger, *Eton of Old or Eighty Years Since (1811-1822)* (London: Griffith Farran & Co. , 1892).

Anonymous, *Guide to Eton: Eton Alphabet; Eton Block; Eton Glossary* (London: Whittaker and Co. , 1861).

Benson, A. C. , *Fasti Etonenses: A Biographical History of Eton* (London: R. Ingalton Drake, 1899).

Byrne, L. S. R. and E. L. Churchill, *Changing Eton: A Survey of Conditions based on the History of Eton since the Royal Commission of 1862-64* (London, Jonathan Cape, 1937).

Byrne, L. S. R., *The Eton Boating Book* (Eton: Spottiswoode, Ballantyne & Co., 1933).

Coleridge, Arthur, *Eton in the Forties* (London: Richard Bentley and Son, 1896).

Elphinstone, Howard Warburton, *Recollections of the Thirties and Forties of the Nineteenth Century* (For Private Circulation: nd).

Gambier-Parry, E., *Annals of an Eton House* (London: John Murray, 1907).

Green, W. C., *Memories of Eton and King's* (Eton: Spottiswoode & Co., 1905).

Hill, M. D., *Eton and Elsewhere* (London: John Murray, 1928).

L'Estrange, A. G., *Vert de Vert's Eton Days* (London:

Elliot Stock, 1887).

Lubbock, Alfred, *Memories of Eton and Etonians* (London: John Murray, 1899).

Luxmoore, H. E., *Letters of H. E. Luxmoore* (Cambridge: Cambridge University Press, 1929).

Lyte, H. C. Maxwell, *A History of Eton College (1440-1910)* (London: Macmillan, 1911).

Maclure, J. Stuart, *Educational Documents: England and Wales, 1816 to present day* (London: Methuen, 1973).

Marten, C. H., *Recollections of an Eton Colleger, 1898-1902* (Eton: Spottiswoode and Co. , 1905).

Nevill, Ralph, *Floreat Etona: Anecdotes and Memories of Eton College* (London: Macmillan, 1911).

O.E., *Eton Under Hornby* (London: A. C. Fifield, 1910)

Parker, Eric, *College at Eton* (London: Macmillan, 1933).

Parker, Eric, *Eton in the 'Eighties* (London: Macmillan, 1914).

Parker, Eric, *Floreat: An Eton Anthology* (London: Nisbet & Co., 1923).

Pawson, John, *The Field Game* (Eton: Spottiswoode, Ballantyne & Co. , 1935).

Salt, Henry Stephens, *Memories of Bygone Eton* (London: Hutchinson & Company, 1928).

Seely, Richard, *A Wartime Education at Aysgarth and Eton* (Eton: 2001).

Stapylton, H.E.C., *The Eton School Lists from 1791 to 1877* (Eton: R.Ingalton Drake, 1885).

The Old Etonian Association, *The Eton Register, Part I, 1841-1850* (Eton: Spottiswoode & Co., 1903).

The Old Etonian Association, *The Eton Register, Part IV, 1871-1880* (Eton: Spottiswoode & Co., 1907).

The Old Etonian Association, *The Eton Register, Part V, 1883-1889* (Eton: Spottiswoode & Co., 1908)

The Old Etonian Association, *The Eton Register, Part VI, 1889-1899* (Eton: Spottiswoode & Co., 1910)

The Old Etonian Association, *The Eton Register, Part VI, 1899-1909* (Eton: Spottiswoode & Co., 1922)

Secondary Sources: Articles and Chapters

Connell, R. W. & J. W. Messerschmidt, 'Hegemoic Masculinity Rethinking the Concept', *Gender and Society*, 19:6 (2005), 829-59.

Francis, Martin, 'The domestication of the male? Recent research on nineteenth-and twentieth-century

British masculinity', *The Historical Journal* 45.3 (2002): 637-652.

Holt, Jenny, 'The Textual Formations of Adolescence in Turn-of-the-Century Youth Periodicals: The "Boy's Own Paper" and Eton College Ephemeral Magazines', *Victorian Periodicals Review*, 35:1 (Spring, 2002), pp. 63-88

Roberts, David, 'The Paterfamilias of the Victorian Governing Class' in *The Victorian Family*, ed. by Anthony S. Wohl (Beckenham: Croom Helm, 1978).

Tosh, John, 'What should historians do with masculinity? : Reflections on nineteenth-century Britain', *History Workshop*, 38 (1994) 179-202.

Secondary Sources: Books

Austen-Leigh, R. A. , *A Guide to Eton College* (Eton: Eton College, 1988).   .

Balston, Thomas, *Dr. Balston at Eton* (London: Macmillan, 1952).

Bamford, T. W. , *Rise of the public schools: a study of boys' public boarding schools in England and Wales from 1837 to the present day* (London: Nelson, 1967).

Benson, Arthur Christopher, *The Diary of Arthur Christopher Benson* (London: Hutchinson, 1926).

Briscoe, John, *555 years of Medical Care at Eton* (Eton: Eton College, 1996).

Card, Tim, *Eton Established: A History from 1440-1860* (London: John Murray, 2001).

Card, Tim, *Eton Renewed: A History from 1860 to the Present Day* (London: John Murray, 1994).

Chandos, John, *Boys Together: English Public Schools 1800-1864* (London: Hutchinson, 1984).

Connell, R. W., Gender and Power (London, 1987).

Connell, R. W., Masculinities (Cambridge, 1995).

Daix, Pierre, *Braudel* (Paris: Flammarion, 1995).

Fletcher, Anthony, *Growing up in England: The Experience of Childhood, 1600-1914* (New Haven and London: Yale University Press, 2008)

Fletcher, C. R. L., *Edmond Warre*, (London: John Murray, 1922).

French, Henry and Mark Rothery, *Man's Estate: Landed Gentry Masculinities 1660-1900* (Oxford: Oxford University Press, 2012).

Gargano, Elizabeth, *Reading Victorian Schoolrooms* (London: Routledge, 2008).

Gathorne-Hardy, Jonathan, *The public school phenomenon, 597-1977* (London : Hodder and Stoughton, 1977).

Green, W. C. , *Memories of Eton and King's* (Eton: Spottiswoode, 1905).

Hendrick, Harry, *Children, Childhood and English Society, 1880-1990* (Cambridge: Cambridge University Press, 1997).

Hewitt, Martin, ed. , *The Victorian World* (London: Routledge, 2012).

Honey, John Raymond de Symons, *Tom Brown's Universe: The Development of the Victorian Public School* (London: Millington, 1977).

Keenan, Debbie and Bobbie Latter, *Windsor: A History* (Salisbury: Francis Frith, 2004).

Lawrence, P.S.H., ed., *The Encouragement of Learning* (Salisbury: Michael Russell, 1980).

Lawrence, P. S. H., *An Eton Camera* (Salisbury: Michael Russell, 1980).

Mack, Edward C., *Public Schools and British Opinion 1780-1860: An Examination of the Relationship between Contemporary Ideas and the Evolution of an English Institution* (London: Methuen, 1938).

Mack, Edward C., *Public Schools and British Opinion Since 1860: The Relationship between Contemporary Ideas and the Evolution of an English Institution* (New York: Columbia University Press, 1941).

Maxwell Lyte, H. C. , *A History of Eton College 1440-*

1910 (London: Macmillan, 1911).

Mangan, James Anthony, *Athleticism in the Victorian and Edwardian Public School: The emergence and consolidation of an educational ideology* (London: Routledge, 2012).

Mangan, James A., and James Walvin, eds., *Manliness and Morality: Middle Class Masculinity in Britain and America, 1800-1940* (Manchester: Manchester University Press, 1987).

Meredith, M. C. *500 years of Eton drama* (Eton: Eton College, 2001).

Money, Tony, *Manly & Muscular Diversions: Public Schools and the Nineteenth-Century Sporting Revival* (London: Gerald Duckworth & Company, 1997).

Musgrave, Peter William, ed., *Society and Education in England since 1800* (London: Routledge, 2013.)

Newsome, David, *Godliness and Good Learning: Four Studies on a Victorian Ideal* (London: John Murray, 1961).

Ogilvie, Vivian, *The English Public School* (London: Batsford, 1957).

Osborne, Richard, *Music & Musicians of Eton* (London: The Cygnet Press, 2012).

Parker, Peter, *The old lie: The Great War and the public-school ethos* (London: Constable, 1987).

Rodgers, John, Old Public Schools of England (New York: Charles Scribner's Sons, 1938).

Roper, Michael and John Tosh, eds. , *Manful Assertions: Masculinities in Britain since 1800* (London: Routledge, 1991).

Rothblatt, Sheldon, *The Revolution of the Dons* (London: Faber and Faber, 1968).

Shrosbree, Colin, *Public Schools and Private Education: the Clarendon Commission, 1861-64, and the Public Schools Acts* (Manchester: Manchester University Press, 1988).

Simon, Brian and Ian Bradley, eds. , *The Victorian public school : studies in the development of an educational institution : a symposium* (Dublin : Gill and Macmillan, 1975).

Stone, Christopher, *Eton* (London: A. & C. Black, 1909).

Thackery, Francis St. John, *Memoir of Edward Craven Hawtrey* (London: George Bell and Sons, 1896).

Tosh, John, *A Man's Place: Masculinity and the Middle-Class Home in Victorian England* (New Haven and London: Yale University Press, 2007).

Tosh, John, 'Domesticity and Manliness in the Victorian Middle Class: The family of Edward White Benson' in *Manful Assertions: Masculinities in Britain since 1800* (London: Routledge, 1991) ed by Roper, Michael and John Tosh.

Vance, Norman, *The Sinews of the Spirit: the Ideal of Christian Manliness in Victorian Literature and Religious Thought* (Cambridge: Cambridge University Press, 1985).

Acknowledgements

At the Open University: Rachel Duffett for guidance on historical research and presentation of findings, and Brian Gurrin for advice over the course of this project.

At Eton College Archives: Penny Hatfield for induction into the use of the archives; Eleanor Cracknell for help throughout this project, finding several useful primary sources for every line of enquiry.

About the Author

H. A. Shirwani has degrees in languages and history,
and has taught at Eton College since 2004.

22987253R00081

Printed in Great Britain
by Amazon